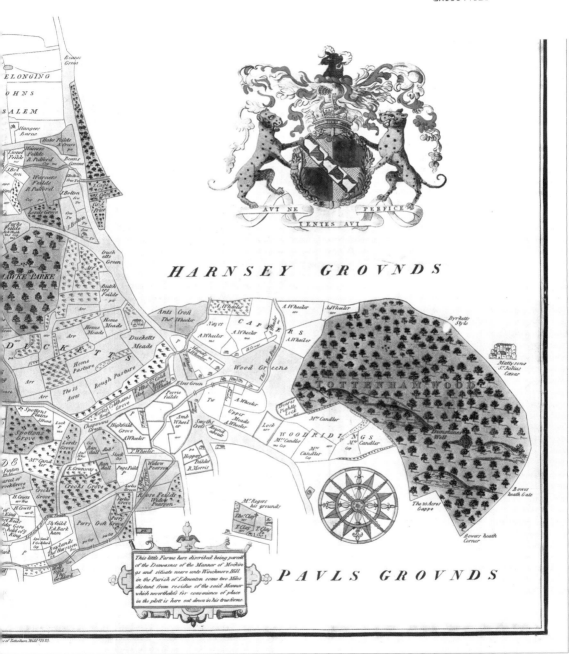

HARNSEY GROVNDS

TOTTENHAM WOOD

PAVLS GROVNDS

AVT NE PERFICE
TENTES AVT

This little Farme here discribed being parcell
of the Demeasnes of the Mannor of Mockin
gs and situate neare unto Winchmore Hill
in the Parish of Edmonton some tvo Miles
distant from residue of the said Mannor
which neverthelesse for convenience of place
in the plott is here set down in his true forme.

TOTTENHAM
A History

Tottenham High Cross *in a 1799 water colour by Samuel Ireland. The High Cross was always a place of significance in the history of Tottenham, although its origins are obscure.*

TOTTENHAM
A History

Christine Protz

PHILLIMORE

2009

Published by
PHILLIMORE & CO. LTD
Chichester, West Sussex, England
www.phillimore.co.uk
www.thehistorypress.co.uk

ISBN 978-1-86077-599-4

Printed and bound in Great Britain

CONTENTS

List of Illustrations

Frontispiece: *Tottenham High Cross* in a 1799 water colour by Samuel Ireland.

ILLUSTRATION ACKNOWLEDGEMENTS

I am grateful to Bruce Castle Museum & Archives of Haringey Culture, Libraries & Learning Service for the use of the majority of images reproduced in this book. I am also grateful to the following for their permission regarding the use of the rest of the images:

George Ioannou, 8; Sylvia Collicott, 11 and 12; Robert Waite, 31, 53; Henry Jacobs, 38.

ACKNOWLEDGEMENTS

I am indebted to many people for their help with the completion of this book. To Annemarie Allan and Lauren Peril for their patience in reading the text, and to Val Crosby, Hazel Whitehouse, Bill Rust, Clare Stephens and others in the Search Room for their help and advice in negotiating the archives. Also to Robert Waite and Claire Wilson for their hard work producing the images for publication. Above all, I wish to thank Deborah Hedgecock, Curator of Bruce Castle Museum, for her assistance with the text and images, despite the many demands on her time. Her knowledge and expertise regarding the range of pictures and artefacts in the Museum collection, as well as the history of the area, have been invaluable in the final production of this book.

To Gladys Annie Claydon

INTRODUCTION

Today Tottenham is submerged in north London, a one-third part of the London Borough of Haringey. It is bound by Wood Green and Hornsey to the west, Stoke Newington and Hackney to the south, Edmonton on the north and Walthamstow eastwards across the River Lea. But for most of its history it was a straggling village separated from the city by the open fields of villages such as Stoke Newington, Dalston and Haggerston.

Tottenham enjoyed a rural environment until the 19th century, when a dramatic population growth, stimulated by the railways, led to the explosion of people out of London's congested streets and into the outlying villages. Tottenham grew rapidly, and with the increase in population its western portion split away to become the independently administered parish of Wood Green in 1888. The 20th century witnessed Tottenham's growth as a town and gradual assimilation into London as the city expanded, eventually to become part of the Borough of Haringey.

But even before the railways, and eventual absorption into London, the capital had a constant effect on the village. Linking Tottenham to the City today is the main artery of the A10 cutting its way northwards through the parish. In the past this was Ermine Street, a Saxon name for the Roman road running from London to the north, and known locally as the High Road and, earlier, as Tottenham Street. This is Tottenham's main thoroughfare, built even before the place came into existence. It was here that the early hamlets of Tottenham High Cross and Tottenham Streete were established.

As well as a link to London, Ermine Street also went north to Lincoln and on to York and Northumberland, and eventually Scotland. These northern lands had a significant effect on the unusual nature of the early lordships of the manor. Although it was on the Saxon side of King Alfred's border with the Danelaw, it was nevertheless possessed by Danish earls in Northumberland. Later, it became one of the English possessions of Scottish kings and nobles until Scotland asserted its independence in 1306 and lost its English lands.

This highway has had a constant effect on the nature of Tottenham's development and its population. The northern lords, and other later manor lords, were attracted to it as a convenient stopping place to and from London. From the 15th century, City merchants chose to build their country houses here, followed in the 18th century by middle-class professionals, with their substantial villas, and eventually, in the late 19th century, lower middle-class and

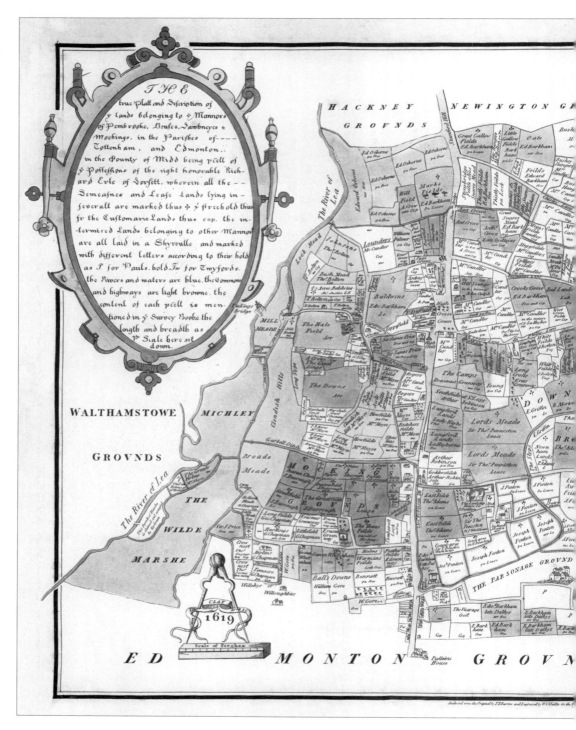

1   *Tottenham in 1619. This map is based on the parish survey authorised by the Earl of Dorset and, unlike most maps, north is at the bottom and south at the top.*

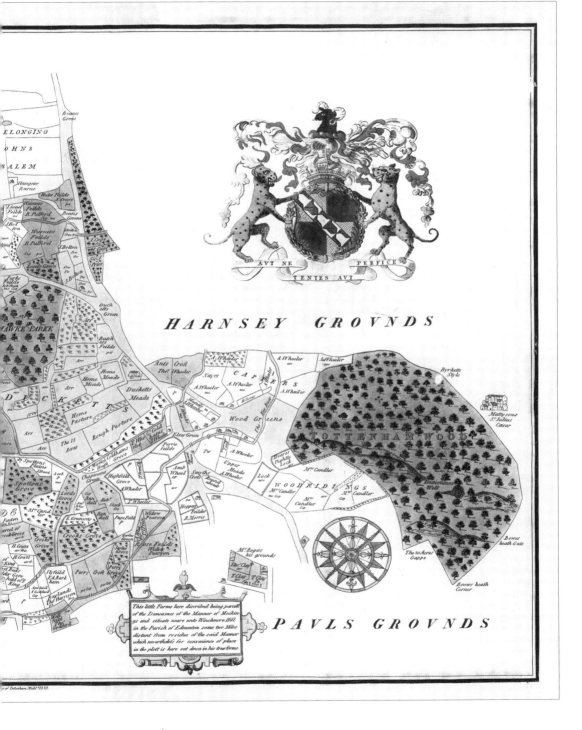

HARNSEY GROVNDS

TOTTENHAM WOOD

PAVLS GROVNDS

AVT NE PERFICE
TENTES AVT

This little Farme here discribed being parcell
of the Demeasnes of the Manner of Mockin
gs and sitiuate neare vnto Winchmore Hill
in the Parish of Edmonton some two Miles
distant from residue of the said Manner
which nevertheless for convenience of place
in the plott is here set down in his true forme.

working-class residents flooded into the newly built terraced streets.

London was also a market for Tottenham produce from the Middle Ages to the 19th century, providing hay and wood (until the last trees disappeared), fattened cattle and eventually plants and vegetables from the market gardens and nurseries. The intractable clay soil also came into its own, producing bricks, pipes and tiles for building, and flowerpots for the nurseries.

Not surprisingly, with so much traffic going through and between the village and London, Tottenham has long been a place of migration. It has attracted people from the rest of the United Kingdom as well as Londoners, and substantial numbers from further afield. French, Spanish, African, Indian, German and Italian residents have been recorded long before the post-war wave of migration.

Written records for Tottenham go back to Domesday, and continue through the Middle Ages with the surviving manor rolls. Some of these rolls have been translated, so giving us access to interesting details regarding life in the village at that time. There have also been a number of histories written about Tottenham, beginning with William Bedwell writing in 1631 what is believed to be one of the first local histories. He was followed by Henry Hare, the 2nd Lord Coleraine, whose unpublished manuscript of 1715 is now housed in the Bodleian Library. Further additions to the manuscript were made by his grandson, also Henry Hare. In 1790 H.G. Oldfield and R.A. Dyson published their more comprehensive history, updating the earlier ones.

The 19th century saw the substantial history of William Robinson, published in 1818, with a later two-volume edition in 1840. Over the following decades a number of other local residents made their contributions with memoirs and stories of old Tottenham. By the 20th century two notable local historians stand out: Fred Fisk and William Roe. Fisk, a local bookseller, photographer and publisher, issued his book in 1913 as well as a postcard series of *Views of Old Tottenham*. William Roe published his well-researched books following the Second World War.

The last few decades have seen a plethora of excellent publications detailing specific events, periods and personalities. Many of these have been published by the Edmonton Hundred Historical Society (which includes Tottenham); others have been commercial and private publications. All of them are detailed in the bibliography, and for any one wishing to follow up specific aspects of Tottenham's history they are well worth reading.

These histories have largely been thematic in approach or confined to one period. The aim of this history is to offer a chronological narrative of Tottenham's past and development, from its origins to the place it is today. Inevitably with such an overview, limited by the demands of space, there have been a few omissions, and I apologise for these in advance. One large omission has been Wood Green, once part of Tottenham, and this is because the history of that parish has been written by Albert Pinching, and his *Wood Green Past* should be seen as a companion volume to this.

I am, of course, grateful to all historians, past and present, who have contributed to our knowledge of Tottenham and to this work. I am particularly grateful to Bruce Castle Museum and Archives, its exceptional collections of documents, publications, photographs and archives, ensuring that, although Tottenham's past may be largely lost, it is not forgotten.

ONE

Road and River – The First Settlements

An early map of Tottenham in 1619 shows many of today's main roads already in use as lanes and highways. White Hart lane, Lordship lane, St Ann's road, West Green road, Philip lane and High Cross lane are there, linking hamlets, fields, church and manor house. Running through the middle from north to south is the High road, part of the main highway from London, and on the western edge is Green Lanes, a drovers road also leading to London. The High road, at one time known as Tottenham Street, was part of an old Roman road, Ermine Street, leading from London to the north. It is probably because of this road that Tottenham first came into existence, and this strategic link with London has affected its growth and development and the nature of its population ever since.

EARLY DAYS

If we are to go back to Tottenham two thousand and more years ago, before settlers had begun to make their dramatic mark on the landscape, we find it was largely covered by dense woodland. To the east the broad River Lea meandered and twisted southwards towards the Thames from Hertfordshire, frequently flooding the low ground where Tottenham eventually appeared. The thickly forested higher land to the west was cut by several streams running down to meet the River Lea in three main tributaries: Pymmes brook in the north east, Stonebridge in the south and the Moselle, the most important of these, travelling an erratic course through the district from the north west to the south east. As well as the streams there were a number of springs which provided wells for later settlers.

The land alongside the Lea produced a rich alluvial soil, whilst the earth lying beneath the woodlands included fertile brickearth in the east, some patches of gravel, and the more difficult to work clay further west. The area had plenty of good arable land, as well as highly productive meadowland which, together with its woodland, could produce a surplus that found a ready market in the ever-expanding city of London, right up to the 20th century. Even the more unwieldy clay later came into its own as a source for making bricks and plant pots.

It was these natural elements, the soil, the woods, the streams and river, plus its closeness to the city, that helped shape the nature of Tottenham's development and its growth as a well-populated settlement.

ROMAN ROAD, SAXON NAME

We can conjecture that the Neolithic people of Britain would have been attracted here by the

2   *A mammoth's tooth found on Tottenham marshes. Mammoths roamed Britain as recently as 14,000 years ago.*

rivers and streams providing water, transport and fishing, as well as the woods for hunting, building and fire. However, their presence, overlaid by later arrivals with their undoubtedly heavier footprint, has been obscured. Most will have been transitory, and have left no evidence of settlements. A Neolithic flint dagger from around 1900-1500 BC has been discovered in the Tottenham area, but with the absence of any pottery remains from the period we must conclude this was more likely to have been left by people passing through rather than settlers.

The one clue to early settlers in Tottenham may be in its name, although there is some difference of opinion here. Various historians have suggested Celtic or Roman origins for the name. Fred Fisk has linked the High Cross with a Celtic god, whilst William Roe has suggested it referred to a Roman mark on the highway. However, the more commonly agreed origin of the name is that it is Saxon. The simplest version is that it comes from a man's name, 'Tota', and 'Ham' refers to a settlement or home. A more complicated version

of this has the 'Tot' part of the name deriving from 'Totia', shaped like a horn, in reference to the shape of Tottenham, but this is more doubtful. The likelihood, though, is that the earliest settlement in Tottenham was Saxon.

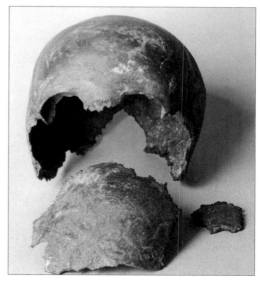

3   *Neolithic skull found in the marshes, evidence of human habitation as far back as the Stone Age.*

The Romans, whether or not they settled here, did have a significant impact on Tottenham. Its location, due north of the Roman city of Londinium, was strategically placed on one of the great Roman roads, running from Bishopsgate in London to Lincoln and York, later called Ermine Street. Some early local historians have disputed whether the Roman road would have followed its usual straight course through Tottenham, citing as a problem the frequent flooding from the western streams as well as the River Lea. They argued that it was more likely to deviate to the west and follow the higher ground closer to the present day Green Lanes. Modern research, however, has now identified Ermine Street as running along, or close by, the modern High Road in Tottenham, deviating a little to the west between Bruce Grove and the border with Edmonton.

We can be certain the Romans passed through Tottenham, but did they settle here? There has been the occasional signs of Roman presence in the area with a few finds of coins and pottery. There is indication of a settlement in Highgate, where the remains of

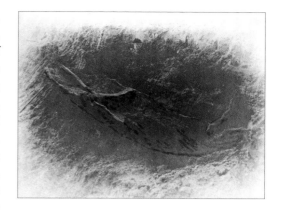

5 *Dug out boat* in situ, *found in 1900 over Tottenham Marshes.*

a Roman kiln have been found, but there is no such evidence in Tottenham. However, the Tottenham historian, William Roe, produced a complicated argument to show that the topography could be interpreted as indicating a Roman presence. Firstly, there are what he refers to as 'marks', possibly relating to the Roman survey of Middlesex. The first mark was a stone, later used as a mounting block, found on the eastern side of the High Road, just south of St Ann's Road. Close to the stone was Markfield House, and it is near an ancient field referred to as Marke Fields in the 1619 map of Tottenham. The 20th-century historian, Sir Montagu Sharpe, writing the history of Middlesex, also connected this mark stone with one directly to the east across the Lea in Walthamstow, on the site of Mark House.

The second mark identified by Roe was the High Cross referred to earlier. Tottenham High Cross, on its raised ground, was first mentioned in 1409, but its origins and purpose remain obscure. The evidence for its role as a Roman mark, like the evidence for its role in the Celtic religion, is not available. However, it is halfway between the south Tottenham mark and a third one discovered by Roe on the Edmonton boundary and mentioned in 13th-century deeds as 'Tottenhammemarke'.

4 *Neolithic tools found in the marshes. They include a hammer with a hole and flint flakes for cutting.*

6   Tottenham High Cross *in a 1799 water colour by Samuel Ireland. The High Cross was always a place of significance in the history of Tottenham, although its origins are obscure.*

William Roe also argued that the land east of Ermine Street was used by the Romans to harvest hay, and that the lines and measurements of old roads and boundaries indicate Roman planning. Certainly he was confident that Romans had surveyed Tottenham, even if the possibility that they used or managed fields in the area is less certain.

AN ANGLO-SAXON SETTLEMENT

By the fourth century, Rome and its empire were under continuous threat from the Germanic tribes of northern Europe. This was a restless, anarchic time, in which towns and cities declined and the wealthy trading city of Londinium was sacked and abandoned. The native Britons of the east and midlands were pushed back under successive waves of invasion, and the population changed from the Celts to the fairer Angles, Saxons and Jutes. New kingdoms were formed, with a different social order and systems of justice and administration. Shires were established, later to become counties, with their sub-divisions of Hundreds, and the Church began to grow in power after the pagan Anglo-Saxons converted to Christianity in the seventh century. These were the developments that helped shape Tottenham, now emerging as a settlement beside the River Lea.

But by the time the warrior tribes of the Anglo-Saxons had settled, there was a further wave of bloody invasions from the Danish Vikings. By the late ninth century, King Alfred, one of the first of the English kings, was desperately fighting to keep and extend his successful Saxon Kingdom of Wessex from the land-hungry Vikings. Following several defeats and significant victories, he reached a settlement with the Danes, keeping them to the eastern shires from the Humber to Essex. The eastern lands were now known as the Danelaw and Tottenham found itself on the frontier between Saxon Wessex and Danish Essex when the River Lea was established as part of the border. According to the Anglo-Saxon Chronicle, in 894 the Danes rowed up the River Lea from the Thames and built a fort on the River at either Ware or Hertford. Alfred then blocked their way out by making the River Lea impassable, whether by erecting fortifications further down or blocking the river is not clear, and the Danes abandoned their fortification and their boats.

Robinson, writing in 1840, claimed that King Alfred's works along the River Lea had the effect of draining the marshes by cutting channels and erecting a 'shass' at Blackwell to block the tide from the Thames. Whatever the truth of the claim, it is clear from their name that the marshes had been boggy, waterlogged land on both sides of the Lea at Walthamstow and Tottenham. Although these fields were still subject to flooding even in the 20th century, by the time of the Domesday Survey of 1086 they had become mainly fertile meadowland, providing hay to meet more than local needs.

But was there a settlement that we can call Tottenham at that time? Written and archaeological evidence is scarce here. It has been suggested a Saxon or Danish homestead was located in present-day Lordship Recreation Ground. An ancient Homestead Moat has been recorded as being situated at a bend in the Moselle, three-quarters of a mile south-west of All Hallows Church. This moat, thought to be where the present pond is located, is perhaps the last remaining visual evidence of the earliest inhabitants in Tottenham.

There is no direct archaeological evidence to indicate a Saxon or Danish settlement, but there are many clues that point to the existence of a farming village by the 10th century. Tottenham, like much of Middlesex, was largely forest over heavy clay soil, and was not attractive farming land for the colonising Saxons. However, parts of Tottenham had good arable soil, and the forest was limited by the watery lands around the Lea.

7 *A diorama of a Saxon-Age settlement showing what early Tottenham might have looked like. We are looking down towards the River Lea.*

It also had good access to fresh water, through streams and springs. Most importantly, it was located on the Roman road, Ermine Street, linking London to the north. By the eighth century London was again a thriving city and the Anglo-Saxon historian, the Venerable Bede, was able to describe it as a 'trading centre for many nations who visit it by land and sea'. Tottenham would have had a role as a place on the route between London and the north, as well as possibly providing some of the wood, food and hay the hungry city needed.

In the 11th century, the Domesday survey provides the first written record of Tottenham. It shows Tottenham had a manor, and was located in the Edmonton Hundred in the county of Middlesex. The manor had belonged to Waltheof, the only English earl to retain his titles after the Norman Conquest, until, with treacheries on all sides, he was eventually executed in 1076 by William. Waltheof, the son of the Danish Siward, Earl of Northumbria, was also Earl of Huntingdon, and Tottenham was part of the Honour of Huntingdon.

It is with Waltheof that we begin to see the emergence of Tottenham's significant characteristics. Firstly, there is the close connection with the Honour of Huntingdon, further north along Ermine Street and one of Alfred's defensive burghs in his war against the Danes. There is also a link with Scotland, as Siward was related to the Scottish royal family and gave protection to Malcolm, son of King Duncan, who was defeated by Macbeth in 1040.

8   *Waltheof, son of Siward, Earl of Northumbria. Waltheof was the first recorded lord of Tottenham Manor. Illustration by George Ioannou.*

Finally, the manor itself was held by a nobleman, and not by the Crown, as, later, were Enfield and Edmonton, or the Church, as was the case with nearby Hornsey and Stoke Newington. These characteristics, together with its position on the main highway of Ermine Street, helped shape the medieval village of Tottenham.

9   *Part of a boat found on the marshes during the building of the reservoirs and identified as Viking. The River Lea was part of the border between the Saxons and the Danes established by King Alfred, and the Vikings were known to have rowed up the river from London to their fortification at either Ware or Hertford.*

1254
TOTTENHAM MANOR DIVIDED

THE MANOR OF BRUCE LATER KNOWN AS FAUCONER	MANOR OF BALLIOLS LATER KNOWN AS DAUBENEYS	MANOR OF HASTINGS LATER KNOWN AS PEMBROKES
Robert de Brus passes to his son and grandson Robert	Devorgild de Baliol	Henry de Hastings
	1281	1269 John, Lord Hastings
1306	John de Balliol, later King of Scotland	1292
Robert Bruce, later King of Scotland	1296	Hugh de Kendale
English lands sequestered by Edward I	Forfeited English lands to crown	1313
Becomes three parts	1308	Laurence, Earl of Pembroke
	John, Earl of Richmond	1348
	1334	John, Earl of Pembroke
TWO-THIRDS MANOR OF BRUCE/FAUCONER	William Daubeney	1375
	1366	Anne, Lady Pembroke
1341	Giles Daubeney	1384
Sir Thomas Hethe	1382	John, Lady Ann's son
1374	John Comberton of Northampton	1389
reverts to the crown then to Edmund de Chesthunte, one of King's falconers	Lands forfeited	Lord Grey of Ruthin
	1384	1397
1397	Lord Beauchamp	Phillipa, John's widow, granted as dower
Robert Fauconer	1388	1401
1398	Forfeited to crown	John Walden and Roger Walden
John Walden	1392	1427
1418	John of Northampton regains lands	Conveyed to John Gedeney
Walden's widow Idony	1409	
1427	William Comberton	
John Gedeney	1412	
	Thomas Burton	
ONE THIRD MANOR OF MOCKINGS	1421	
	Richard Comberton	
1335	1426	
Richard Spigurnell	Richard Chippenham and others	
1340	1449	
John Mocking		
1348		
Nicholas Mockings		
1360		
coheirs Margaret and Idony		
1363		
Elmingus (Helming) Leget		
1397		
son Elmingus		
1427	1449	
mortgaged to John Gedeney	John Gedeney died seized of the four manors	

14   *Chart of the medieval manors of Tottenham, showing the succession through the Scottish royal family to the division into three manors and, finally, reunification with John Gedeney.*

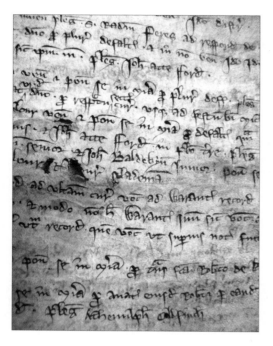

15 *Extract from the Tottenham manorial rolls of 1318, the earliest surviving court roll.*

Chesthunte, one of the king's falconers, and after that became known as Fauconers. The Bruce manor house was probably situated in the same area as present-day Bruce Castle, where medieval foundations have recently been identified.

Balliols manor became Daubeneys following 1334, when it was granted to William Daubeney, and Hastings became Pembrokes from the 14th century. Pembroke manor house was probably along White Hart Lane where the later Rectory House was located.

All these manors were reunited in the 15th century following purchases by John Gedeney of London, although they were still usually referred to by their old names.

TOTTENHAM REUNITED

During much of the Middle Ages, Tottenham was divided and parcelled out to various lords, parts of it occasionally reverting back to the king. But by the middle of the 15th century,

just as the manorial system as it functioned in our area was drawing to a close, Tottenham was again reunited under one lord, a commoner who lived in his manor house in Tottenham during his later years. So who was John Gedeney?

Gedeney was a City merchant and representative of an class of people who were increasingly making their homes in the more pleasant countryside of Tottenham, away from the stew of the City streets. He played his part in the civic administration of the less than orderly City of the 15th century, sometimes reluctantly. When he was first elected in 1415 by the inhabitants of Farringdon he refused the post, probably because he wanted to build up his business. The response of the Mayor and Alderman was to imprison him, shut his houses and sequester all his goods. He accepted office, and went on to be an Alderman until his death in 1469. He also served a term as sheriff and two as mayor.

In spite of holding these offices, it seems Gedeney did not play a very active part in the governance of London. He did, however, expend considerable energy in developing his drapery business, becoming the principal supplier of cloth for the liveries of the Grocers' Company, and included the royal household as his clients under Henry V and Henry VI. He expanded his business to import luxury goods from Italy, and also played a prominent part in the Drapers' Company, first as Warden and later as Master when it became incorporated.

Although Gedeney was actively involved in the commerce and administration of London, he had a considerable impact on Tottenham. Firstly, he gradually bought, or otherwise obtained, the various Tottenham manors and reunited them. The acquisition would have given him status and property in the countryside and, in addition, there was an income to be gained from the various fines imposed on local villagers under the feudal system. Secondly, there was

Demesne	Land held in the Lord's personal possession, or exploited directly by the Lord as a 'home farm'
Frenchman	Non-noble immigrant, usually a peasant settler of free status
Hides	A standard unit of assessment for tax, notionally the amount of land which would support a household divided into four virgates. A hide was calculated at 120 acres of arable land. Meadowland, woodland and pasture is additional
Carucates	Used in the north and east of the country (and Tottenham) as a unit of assessment instead of hide
Ploughs/ ploughteams	
Virgate	One quarter of a hide
Villein	Peasant of higher economic status
Bordar	Peasant of lower economic status than a villager
Cottars	Peasant, probably of lower economic status than a smallholder
Vill	A unit of local administration; an area of land that could contain more than one settlement
Slaves	Often translated as serfs, they were usually assigned to the Lord's ploughteam
Woodland	Identified by the number of pigs it could support
Tithing	Ten men over age of 12 attending the manor court

16 *Glossary of terms used in the Domesday extract.*

the opportunity to acquire land, which was used increasingly as pasture to fatten up sheep and cattle for the London market. Thirdly, and perhaps most importantly, he established early industry in Tottenham, with a fulling mill on the River Lea processing woollen cloth, and a brickworks turning the heavy clay into bricks.

THE MANORIAL ROLLS

Tottenham is fortunate in that many of the manor rolls recording the proceedings of the Tottenham courts still survive. Several have been translated from the Latin and are useful

resources as an insight into this period. There were two courts, the Court Baron dealing mainly with land transfers and various transgressions of villagers, and the Court Leet, or View of Frankpledge, for local crimes and wrongdoings such as fights, thefts and debts. The villagers attending these courts were members of a 'tithing', a group of some ten men over the age of 12 who took collective responsibility for the behaviour of the people they represented. They had to pay a fine for attendance, and were also fined if any wrongdoers failed to pay.

The manor rolls we have for the 14th and 15th centuries show a village community largely

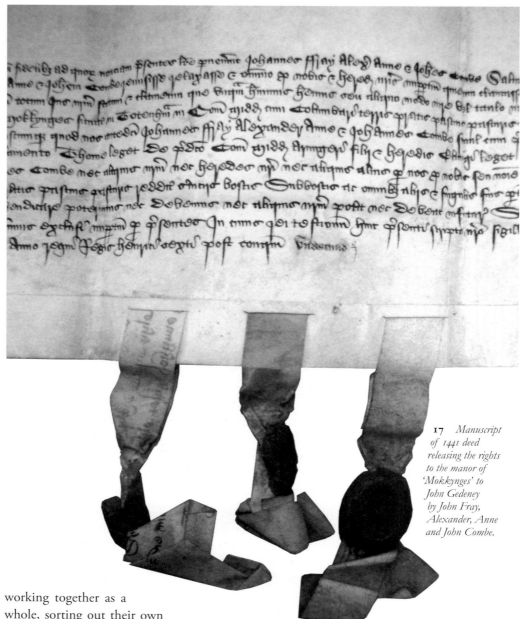

17 *Manuscript of 1441 deed releasing the rights to the manor of 'Mokkynges' to John Gedeney by John Fray, Alexander, Anne and John Combe.*

working together as a whole, sorting out their own crimes, rents and taxation, with varying degrees of oversight from the lord's steward. They indicate what crimes and misdemeanours were committed and (by the size of the fine) how seriously they were viewed. The fines were a source of income for the manor lord, as well as a way of exerting control over villagers.

THREE

Life and Death in a Medieval Manor

What do we know about Tottenham in the 14th and 15th centuries? There were increasing numbers of gentry and tradesmen from London living here, but the bulk of the inhabitants were peasants. They were farmers, but many also had other roles that helped with the smooth running of the village community, such as the Hayward for the marshes and the Woodward for the woods. The Reeve had a particularly onerous job, and was accountable to the lord for work on demesne land, collecting rents and ensuring court orders were followed. The village community nominated people for this post, but the lord's steward usually made the final decision, as in 1392 when the steward rejected John Absolom as 'not sufficient in person nor in wisdom'.

Increasing tension between the needs of the lord and his manor and those of the tenants made the reeve's job an unpopular one and there are a number of references to individuals resisting the post when nominated. In 1387, for example, Robert Reygate was elected reeve of Bruce Manor but refused the post, although he was ordered by the court 'once, twice, thrice' under penalty of a heavy fine of 6s. 8d. He still refused, and 'his goods and chattels, lands and tenement' were 'seized into the lord's hands for

abstaining'. Not surprisingly, he later relented and took the oath. Some nominated reeves, such as William Malger in 1386, came to an arrangement with the steward by paying a hefty fine to be excused: 'John Goodhewe and William Malger are elected for reeves by the homage from whom the lord will elect; and the aforesaid William gives to the lord a fine of 40d., and the aforesaid John is admitted as reeve.'

Some village occupations were carried out in addition to work on the land, such as brewing and selling beer. The early rolls record long lists of men and women fined for 'breaking the assize' for brewing and selling ale and one fined for both brewing and baking. These occupations gradually became full-time, and later in the century we find references to an 'ale-house keeper' and at least one full-time brewer, Thomas Kyng. He probably ran his ale-house along the main street, the 'king's highway', for passing as well as local trade.

Whereas brewing could often be carried out on a casual basis, the village baker required more capital in the form of an oven. The bakers were often more powerful members of the community, especially if they also ran the mill. One baker who stands out from the rolls in the latter part of the 14th century was William Bakere. He appears to have been a dominant, probably aggressive man, frequently in disputes with neighbours. He was also involved in a number of loans and mortgages, usually lending rather than borrowing. Bakere was not always a popular member of the community and when the court found him deficient in his loaves of white bread he was fined the unusually high sum of 16s. 8d. as well as being punished in the pillory.

Bakere was in particular trouble with the whole village in 1383 when he attempted – successfully it seems – to establish a monopoly by taking over another baker's house owned by the brewer Thomas Kyng. The court declared 'that there were three bakers serving the commonalty of the vil and they have gone out of the service of the commonalty, and William Bakere and Robert Baker, out of great malice have driven John Baker, one of them, out of his mansion and conspired to prevent him from his office, therefore the said William and Robert are in mercy by the judgment of the court'.

CHURCH, CHARITY AND CRYPT

The church was central to village life at this time. The parish church of All Hallows (originally known as All Saints) is first recorded in 1132 in a charter of David I of Scotland, when he conveyed the church of Tottenham, together with tithes for its upkeep, to the Augustinian Canons of Holy Trinity, Aldgate. The charter does not refer to the foundation or dedication of the church, so it must have already been in existence from the previous century. The church itself was built on the higher land above the main thoroughfare, and close by the likely position of the manor house. The present building has gone through many periods of repair, addition and reconstruction, and little of the original medieval building remains. It is an uneasy mix of brick and the more ancient stone, with the stone base of the tower likely to be the oldest, probably dating from the Normans. The western end of the nave remains as part of a period of considerable rebuilding in the 14th century, and later, around 1500, the south porch was added, with a room at the top. This room served a number of purposes over the centuries, as a priest's room, an almshouse for the elderly or infirm, and even a school room and, later, a room for children's classes on Sunday.

The first recorded vicar was Robert de Morden in 1327, but there is an earlier reference to a Walter of Tottenham in a deed dated 1254. In this, Henry III entrusts the hospital of St Laurence of Clayhangre to Walter on condition that services are 'creditably and honourably' performed in the hospital chapel.

18 *Medieval jug found in Scotland Green by the High Road.*

Walter has been identified as the Tottenham priest during this period, but the location of the hospital of St Laurence is not clear. There is a Clayhangre on the southern boundary of Tottenham and we also know from manorial rolls that there was a hospital (spitelhouse) probably located south of St Ann's Road, but the name St Laurence is not recorded.

Tottenham was not an ecclesiastical manor, but the church was still a considerable landowner and tenant in this period. The Parsonage and vicarage lands around the church itself covered a good part of the best land around Lordship Lane and White Hart Lane. In the south there were the lands belonging to Clerkenwell Abbey in Tottenham Hanger. These were granted in 1136 by William the Lion (then the Scottish lord). The Clerkenwell lands increased in size over the next three centuries, and other ecclesiastical landowners appear on the scene, such as

19 *The rood tower, All Hallows parish church. The church was conveyed in 1132 to the Augustinian Canons of Aldgate by a charter from King David of Scotland, and the stone base is believed to date from Norman times.*

Charterhouse, St Mary without Bishopsgate and St Bartholomew, Smithfield. Much of this land was obtained by gifts made to the church by lay people, sometimes to secure prayers after their death.

We also find references in the 15th and 16th century to a hermitage at Tottenham High Cross. It appears to have been a small building, perhaps a one room cell, and may have been the residence of a hermit or recluse. There is a record of Henry VIII in 1517 giving 'to father hermit at Totneham 6/8'. The name of the Hermitage

persists, but by the 17th century this had become a 'pretty house' for a family. High Cross was a place of growing importance in Tottenham, located on a rise on the High Road and linked by road eastwards to Tottenham Hale, with its mills and ferry to Walthamstow, and westwards to Green Lanes. By the 15th century it had become a hamlet, vying in importance with the main Tottenham village at the northern end of the High Road.

It is here, at this convenient location, that Tottenham's market was probably held. The

20   *Engraving of All Hallows church made in 1750.*

market is referred to on a couple of occasions in the manor rolls, but little else is known about it, or even if it actually existed. It probably met a mainly local need during the Middle Ages, but would have fallen foul of the London merchants who first ensured all markets within a five mile radius of London were suppressed, then in the 17th century persuaded James I to suppress all markets in a seven mile radius. This would certainly have applied to a market in Tottenham and led to its demise.

QUARRELLING NEIGHBOURS

The courts were where the manor lord, through his steward, could exert his control over tenants and punish them as appropriate, but it was also where petty crime and disputes between neighbours were settled. There are stories of housebreaking, robbery and fights, as well as valuable animals being stolen. The fights usually drew blood and knives were often used. On one occasion a fight led to a death when John Fawkener killed John Jonge in 1380. The trial took place in a higher court, probably Newgate, but as the crime was within the manor, the manor court was able to acquire Fawkener's possessions, worth 39s. It is possible he was hanged at the gallows on Stamford Hill.

Many of the cases before the court concerned the clearance of ditches. This was important in a place like Tottenham which was vulnerable to flooding. When Geoffrey Thurkyll's clogged ditch could take no more water it flowed 'into the king's way to the annoyance of travellers', and the same court declared that Richard Garlaund's unscoured ditch was 'an annoyance of the whole country'. It may have been that 1393 was particularly bad for flooding, or perhaps ditches may have been neglected for a while, because 63 people were fined that year for not clearing their ditches. No one was exempt, including the Prioress of Clerkenwell, the lords of Bruce and Daubeney manors, and the local rector Roger Walden (later Bishop of London). William Bakere was at this court and objected to the fines, declaring the steward untrustworthy and speaking against him. He was fined 6s. 8d. for the outburst.

As well as floods, travellers on the High Road (the king's way) had to contend with dunghills and pits created by nearby households. John Yongewyne was particularly offended by one pit in the High Road as it was next to his gate. The court dealt with these cases through fines, but it is unlikely to have resolved matters permanently.

Animals trespassing on other people's land, or too many animals grazing on the commons, became a particular problem towards the end of the 14th century. Meat consumption was increasing nationally and Tottenham was

a convenient place for fattening livestock for the London market, as we can see from the high number of butchers recorded in the rolls by the beginning of the 15th century. There was not enough meadow and pasture at this time to accommodate the numbers of sheep and cattle coming into the village, and tensions were created when these animals crowded onto the commons or trampled on crops. People were accused of overburdening the commons with sheep 'of foreign vills', and 15 people were called to account in 1391 for allowing their sheep and cattle to trespass on the lord's meadow. William Bakere, again, was accused by Geoffrey Egepol of destroying five acres of corn with his sheep.

TURBULENT TIMES

The 14th century was a troubled time of war, famine, plague and revolt, and the greatest of

21 *Engraving of High Cross with the Hermitage (and hermit), as imagined by Henrietta Townsend in the 18th century.*

these disasters was the Black Death of 1348. There is no direct reference to this in Tottenham, except for the sudden, and shocking, recital of empty tenancies recorded in the Daubeney rolls of May 1348. It opens with 'The tenement which was of John Lece remains in the hands of the lord', and then goes on to list the names of 15 tenants who have died. One would normally expect three or four. Significantly, only five of the empty holdings were re-granted to another tenant, leaving ten empty where apparently there were no heirs in the family left alive to claim them. It has been estimated that perhaps one in seven of the tenants died following this first great plague.

Although there are no clear references to the plague in the manor rolls, the scarcity of labour and changes in feudal relationships affecting the country also occurred in Tottenham. Tensions were especially noticeable towards the end of the 14th century, when the manor rolls show the lords constantly reasserting their rights to submission and loyalty from their tenants in the face of increasing demands for more freedom from feudal restraints. Villagers, tied to the manor from birth, wanted their freedom to leave. There were opportunities for other trades and employment outside Tottenham that would release them from servile labour and local men were increasingly on the move. Five men in 1392 went to live outside the village 'disclaiming to be the lord's villeins'. Three stayed free, but two others were captured and imprisoned in Shoreditch. After much pressure they 'acknowledged themselves to be the lord's villeins' and were 'allowed' to return home. Another villager, Walter Abraham, a currier, was brought to court for being 'in rebellion' by living outside the lordship without permission, and not paying homage. He 'acknowledged himself to be the lord's villein by blood and asks grace of the lord that he might remain at London at

22 Tottenham Marshes, *by A. Legge, 1906. Much of the pasture and meadow of the marshes remained unchanged over the centuries, with hay the most important produce.*

23   *Workmen digging clay for making flower pots at South's Pottery in White Hart Lane. The clay soil was difficult to work*
for agriculture, but was exploited from at least the Middle Ages to make bricks, tiles, pipes and pots.

his trade'. This was agreed on condition that he came to court every year for seven years and paid 'chevage', a fine of 5s. annually.

In 1377 there appears to have been some collective action from the villagers when they refused to reveal the whereabouts of two fugitives, and again in 1378 when they all refused to take the lord's wood to London. Three other men refused to do customary work on the lord's land. These were the years immediately preceding the Peasants Revolt of 1381.

THE FOUNDATION OF MODERN TOTTENHAM

These turbulent years led to a very changed Tottenham in the 15th century. John Gedeney united the manors and set about making them profitable, recording record surpluses. The less than satisfactory clay soil now turned to a more profitable yield through pasture and meadow land, the grazing sheep providing both meat and wool. The latter was processed by Gedeney's fulling mills (two were established on the River

Lea), and the heavy clay itself used to make bricks from his kiln. In 1437/8, 22,000 'breeks' were sold, rising to 52,000 the following year. There was a ready and ever-hungry market in London for all the meat, wool, cloth, bricks and hay.

Manorial land was increasingly rented out and customary services commuted to money payments or quit rents, and peasant holdings were gradually evolving to free copyhold. As land was sold, and changed hands, many of the scattered strips were consolidated into larger units. Increasing attempts were made – some successful, some not – to enclose land into farming units. Many of the long established family names begin to disappear from the rolls, either moving out of the manor or dropping out of sight by becoming landless cottagers, some doubtless working in the fulling mills or brickworks. Many new occupations are recorded, including a saddler, tailor, mason, surveyor, cap maker, goldsmith, draper, barber and currier, as well as brewers and bakers. Some

24   *The mills on the River Lea used the water power for making cloth as well as flour. When this early 19th-century engraving was made for Robinson's* History and Antiquities of the Parish of Tottenham, *they also manufactured leather and paper.*

of these new Tottenham residents may have retired from a London trade, but others were still producing goods for a local and London market, or engaged in passing trade with the traffic on the High Road.

The Kings Highway – the High Road – had become a busy thoroughfare from London to the north, transporting people and goods by foot, horseback and wagon, both in and out of the City. Although it was to be several centuries before the high road became anything other than a muddy track, attempts were continually being made to improve it along its length and keep it in repair. But an amenity that featured early on were the inns and taverns, providing food, drink and shelter. Names such as the *George*, the *Lyon*, the *Tabard* and the *Swan* start to appear, some with gardens attached, and these had become an established feature of Tottenham life by the 15th century.

25   *Levi Jennings, the farriers next to the* George and Vulture *in the High Road. The blacksmith's forge was essential on this highway with its ever-increasing traffic, especially where inns provided a stopping place, and this 19th-century picture shows a scene that changed little over the years.*

Four

Mapping the Manors: Mysteries and Discoveries

… they seem to the traveller to be one continuous street, especially Tottenham and Edmonton, and in all of them the new buildings so far exceed the old … There is not anything more fine in their degree than most of the buildings this way; only with this observation they are generally belonging to the middle sort of mankind grown wealthy by trade, and who still taste of London; some of them live both in the city and in the country at the same time, yet many of these are extremely wealthy.

(Daniel Defoe,
Tour Through England and Wales)

Early in the 17th century Richard Sackville, Duke of Dorset, commissioned a survey of his lands across the country, including Tottenham. The Tottenham survey detailed the names of people who leased or possessed land and the location of their holdings. From this report a map was compiled giving a picture of the roads, fields, streams, woods and houses in the village in 1619, and showing much of the change that had taken place since the 15th century. The map demands some reorientation on the part of the modern viewer as the top points south – towards London – instead of the more usual north, and the east is on the left with the west on the right. With this difficulty in mind, however, the map clearly shows the way Tottenham has developed around the highway from London.

Two villages are shown on the map, both along the high road. Tottenham Street is in the north near the border with Edmonton and, further south, Tottenham High Cross is close to the junctions with the lanes leading west to Walthamstow and east to Green Lanes. Between these villages a number of houses have sprung up, so it appeared to Daniel Defoe as he passed through '… that they seem to the traveller to be one continuous street'. Away from the High Road we can identify the two hamlets of Tottenham Hale in the east and Wood Green over to the west.

Crossing the parish are a number of roads and lanes trodden out by inhabitants over the years as they made their way to fields, church, manor house and the mill. These by-ways can still be found today on modern maps, their names usually changed, but the routes substantially the same.

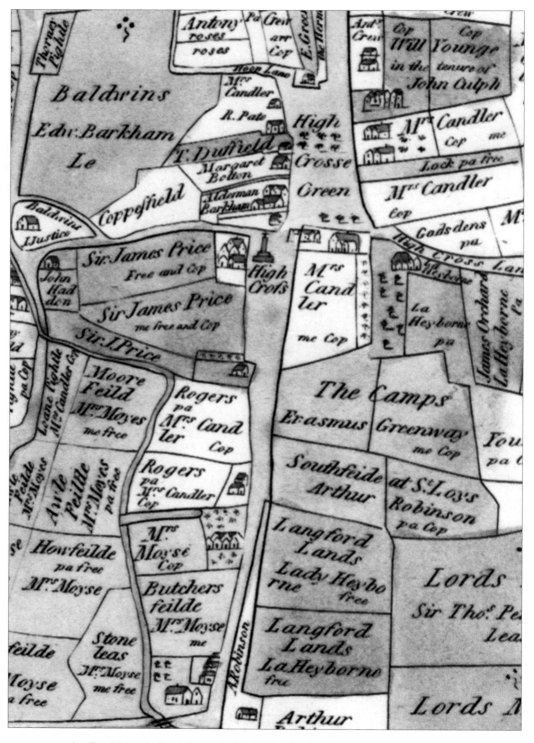

26 *Detail from 1619 Dorset Survey showing the High Road, with houses strung out along its length.*

The Disappearing Commons

Although to our modern eyes this map presents a rural scene of open fields and woods, in fact by 1619 the village was far less 'open' than other contemporary villages around the country. One of the most striking features of the map is that it shows Tottenham almost completely enclosed, with boundaries around its fields, houses, gardens and woods. Very little of the common land used by villagers for farming or animal grazing remains to be seen here in the early 17th century, with inevitable social consequences for the landless poor.

Tottenham's medieval division into many small fields, rather than the more usual three or four larger ones, may have contributed to early enclosures, but the policy of successive manor lords in leasing out demesne land rather than farming it themselves helped, as did their strongly commercial approach to the manor for profit. A manor that encouraged enclosure would have been a more attractive proposition to wealthy Londoners, whether they farmed or lived here themselves or rented the land out.

Most of the remaining common land is in the less densely populated west, with Wood

27 *Sir Hugh Myddleton, whose New River Company constructed the watercourse that brought fresh water from Hertfordshire to Clerkenwell.*

Green Common the largest, followed by Ducketts, Beanes and Elses Greens and Smiths Cross, with its modern-sounding 'roundabout'. But even Wood Green Common has been

28 *Asplins farm in 1907, first identified by name in the 1619 survey, was still a working farm well into the 20th century.*

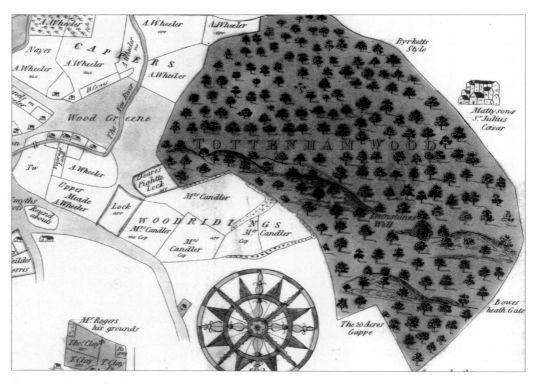

29   *Detail from 1619 Dorset Survey showing the extent of Tottenham Wood, with the New River curling through Wood Green common.*

30   *The timber frames of the old Bull inn exposed in 1939. Much of Tottenham's woodland went towards buildings such as this.*

affected by change, as we can see from the appearance of the New River, emerging from 'Harnsey Grounds' and curving northwards. Built between 1609 and 1613, it was designed to bring fresh water from Hertfordshire to Clerkenwell to tackle the shortage of clean water in the overcrowded city. The project was engineered by Sir Hugh Myddleton and his New River Company, with substantial support from King James I (and VI of Scotland). The company acquired a considerable amount of land in the west of the manor, which was subsequently leased or rented to local landowners, resulting in the loss of more woodland in that area.

The east, in keeping with its later development, is more poorly represented by commons. The High Road manages to keep three small greens, the most substantial being High Cross, whilst two more greens (Hangars and West Green) appear on its western side. Most of the remnants of common land were along the lanes and highway (and referred to as 'waste' by the survey) with the commons scattered along them. Even this land, however, was subject to encroachment from enclosure, particularly along the High Road, although sometimes this was resisted, as when Jaspher Phesaunt was prevented from trying to enclose a common path at the back of his house in 1541. Where rights of way were not an issue, many pieces of land were enclosed with the court's permission along the highway and other lanes, as well as larger areas of land. In this way the houses built along the High Road and other lanes acquired enclosed gardens, so much a feature of Tudor life, as well as orchards and – for the inns and taverns – arbours and pleasure gardens for the relaxation of guests.

Although the hay meadows on the marshes were farmed in common by several landowners before being thrown open to cattle after haymaking, there were also enclosures here.

Asplins farm in the north was probably on the site of one of the earliest settlements on the marshes as they were gradually drained. It had a long history, surviving railways and house building in the 19th century, until its final demise in the twentieth. At this stage in its history one of its fields is shown as a 'garden of roses', the first example of market gardening in this area.

The Last of the Great Forest

As the common lands across Tottenham were being enclosed, we can also see Tottenham's woodland disappearing. The map shows several woods on the very western edge of the parish, the last remaining pieces of the forest. The biggest is Tottenham Wood, jutting out in the west and almost isolated from the rest of Tottenham. This wood, together with Hawkes

31 *The round tower at Bruce Castle, built in Tudor times, still survives today, having been retained by successive lords of the manor for its interesting antiquity. Photograph by Robert Waite.*

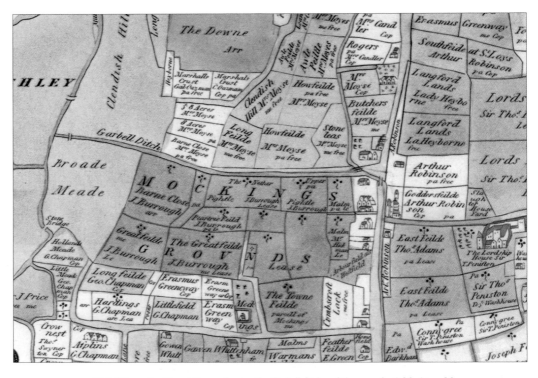

32   Detail from 1619 Dorset Survey showing the Garbell ditch and the grounds of Mockings Manor.

Park, Spottons Grove and Lord's Grove, were all part of the lord's demesne. A few smaller woods belonged to individual wealthy residents, such as Cooks Grove, which was part of Edward Barkham's estate, and the various groves in Duckett's manor. Being privately owned, they were not for the use of ordinary residents. The right to let a certain number of pigs into the woods for 'pannage', where they could root for acorns, seems to have disappeared by the 16th century, and of course there was no question of poaching. The game – deer, pheasant and partridge – was for hunting by the wealthy landowners and friends, as well as, on occasions, the king. James I enjoyed his hunting, but one outing in 1623 to Tottenham Wood was spoilt by the lack of accessible gates in the fences which caused him 'much inconvenience' and led to a stern letter being written to Lady Heybourne and Sir Edward Barkham, leading

local residents demanding gates for easier entry, together with his own personal key for when the gates were locked.

In theory the woodland should have been protected and managed by the woodward to ensure that trees cut down for timber were coppiced and young trees left standing. But wood – like coal, oil and gas in modern times – was a desperately needed commodity, both for fuel and building. Most houses, barns and stables in the district were wood built, bricks being too expensive, and the only locally available fuel for heat and cooking was wood. The local courts regularly tried to intervene but were often too late, or were powerless in the face of a manor lord seeking profit at the expense of the vill. Sir John Risley, lord of the manor from 1507 to 1512, felled and sold more than 160 acres of Tottenham Wood over the four years prior to his death.

THE KING AT 'MAISTER COMPTON'S HOUSE'

The individual houses of the more important inhabitants are shown on the map, and perhaps the most significant of all is the Lordship House on Berry Lane, now known as Bruce Castle, and pictured complete with the tower we see today. It is described in the survey as having barns, stables, a dovehouse, orchard and garden, covering some five acres. The house was built around 1570 by Henry, Lord Compton, grandson of Sir William Compton who had refurbished the original buildings soon after he was granted the Tottenham manors by King Henry VIII in 1513. It seems likely the tower was also built then, and although its purpose is unclear it could have been used as a spectator tower to watch hunting, or even jousting, or as a hawk mews and possibly even a banqueting hall.

William Compton was a member of the royal household and a favourite of Henry VIII and, although he had properties elsewhere, he undoubtedly lived some of the time in Tottenham. His daughter is buried in the parish church. It would have been a useful place, offering a rural retreat from the crowds and pestilence of London, but still convenient for the court. Its position on the road to the north was also an advantage, and it was at 'Maister Compton's house' in 1516 that the historian Robinson describes Henry VIII greeting his sister, Margaret, widow of King James IV of Scotland, before travelling in glorious procession onwards from Tottenham High Cross to London. Henry VIII also visited another friend in Tottenham on occasion, Sir George Henningham (d.1536), who lived in the Black House near White Hart Lane. By 1619 this house, described as 'sumptuous' in

33   *The* George and Vulture *inn, home to Balthazar Sanchez. Elizabethan coins were discovered under the building when it was pulled down in 1830.*

34   *Sanchez Almshouses from an engraving in Robinson's* The History and Antiquities of the Parish of Tottenham, *published in 1840.*

the survey, is called Rydley on the map and owned by Alderman William Gore.

Compton died of an infectious disease that ravaged London and the court in 1528. His six-year-old son and heir Peter became the ward of Cardinal Wolsey, whose staff included Thomas Cromwell and Sir William Paulet. Under the stewardship of these two astute men, the Tottenham manors prospered as commercial enterprises. Peter died aged 19, before he could reach his majority, leaving a son, Henry, born posthumously to Peter by his young wife Anne Talbot.

Henry Compton became Baron Compton and died in 1589, when Tottenham was held by his second wife, Anne, as a dower. She married Robert Sackville in 1592 and over the following years the manors were passed through members of the Sackville family, variously sold or mortgaged at times to pay off their owner's debts, eventually coming to Hugh Hare, Lord Coleraine, in 1626.

THE MANORS OF DUCKETTS AND MOCKINGS

The map shows two important sub-manors, Ducketts in the south west and Mockings in the north east. Duckets was formed by land purchase from the 13th century, and was separate from the main manors. It was eventually acquired in the mid-15th century by Richard Sturgeon, who built a chapel at St Bartholomew's Hospital in London. After his death he bequeathed the Duckett lands to the hospital for the support of a chantry priest. Following the Reformation, Ducketts was separated from St Bartholomew's and sold to Richard Cecil in 1547.

The sub-manor of Mockings was on the north-east of the High Street close to the marshes. Although Mockings was now part of the united manors of Tottenham following Gedeney's purchase, it still retained its separate identity and in 1619 it was occupied by John Burroughs, gentleman. In 1619 the Mockings

Grounds are bordered by the high street on the west and the marshes on the east, with the Garbell ditch at the southern end and Marsh Lane on the north. The manor house was located along Marsh Lane and is described in the survey as having a moat, garden, two orchards, two barns, a stable and oat house. The manor itself had fields of arable and pasture, as well as hay and meadow land in the marshes, and even some land in neighbouring Edmonton.

The Rectory Manor of Tottenham

Church lands were only obliquely referred to in the manor documents, and this survey is no exception. We can identify the fields in the north belonging to St Paul's (P), the large segment of land in the south west referred to as belonging to St John of Jerusalem, and the extensive Parsonage grounds, with a splendid house rivalling the lordship in size. But the century preceding had been tumultuous times for the church. Following the Reformation vast estates across the country accrued to Henry VIII, to be used for income or gifts to friends, or sales to help finance his wars and pleasures.

In Tottenham the church patronage was taken away from the Augustinian canons of Holy Trinity, Aldgate in 1531. The lesser tithes of the parish always remained with the vicar for his support and the upkeep of the church, but the land and the great tithes were normally leased out, including the Parsonage and its grounds.

35 *The Barkham family memorial in All Hallows church, showing Sir Robert Barkham, his wife Maria, their eight daughters and four sons. Sir Robert was one of the sons of Sir Edward Barkham, a tax collector during the English Civil War.*

36   *The Candeler family tomb in All Hallows church,
showing Richard and Elizabeth Candeler. Elizabeth was
the daughter of the Locke family, who owned considerable
amounts of land in Tottenham during the 15th century.*

After a period in which the Rectory manor passed
from Crown to nobles, it was finally granted to
the Dean and Chapter of St Paul's in 1541.

MONASTIC LAND

Following the dissolution of the monasteries,
Clerkenwell Abbey, St Bartholomew's in
Smithfield and St Mary's without Bishopsgate
no longer had a presence in Tottenham. An
apparently religious order possessing land in
Tottenham which appears for the first time is
St John of Jerusalem in the extreme south-west
corner. This Priory in Clerkenwell became a
secular possession of the Crown and the
Tottenham land appears to have been that
previously held by Clerkenwell Abbey, which
had close connections to the Priory.

Monastic land in Tottenham had become
secular, although this made little difference
to the local population. The exception was a
small hospital that had been established on the
east of the High Street by a gift from Thomas
Billingham and entrusted to St Mary's without
Bishopsgate. It disappeared with the dissolution,
but half a century later that is where we find
the equally charitable Sanchez Almshouses.

'A SUMPTUOUS FAIR HOUSE'

Houses large and small are scattered across
this map, but particularly so along the High
Road where we find the 'mansion houses' of
the wealthy London merchants noted by Daniel
Defoe. There are also the smaller homes of
tradesmen and scholars and the almshouses for
the elderly, as well as the smithies and inns for
travellers along the main highways. There were
several substantial inns along the High Road,
such as the *Lamb* and the *Horns* between White
Hart Lane and Edmonton, and the *Bull* and
the *Swan* at High Cross Green. Some of these
inns, such as the *Swan*, also provided pleasure
gardens for visitors, as well as accommodation
for travellers. Others were new developments,
probably enlarged to take guests. The *George and
Vulture*, for instance, appears to have been built
on the site of the house of Balthazar Sanchez
(d.1602), and was described as having a pleasure
garden, bowling green, fish pond and stabling
for many horses. According to Robinson, writing
a century later, this inn was 'much frequented
by citizens of London taking recreation'.

It is possible that Sanchez was still resident
in the *George and Vulture* when it was an inn,
perhaps as the innkeeper, as there is evidence
it was in existence in Elizabethan times. The
Spaniard had been sweetmaker and confectioner
to Philip II of Spain and in 1554 followed him
to England with Queen Mary during her brief
reign. His trade was a profitable one and he
became a London citizen, retiring to Tottenham
where he was clearly at home. In his will of 1599
he left a bequest of money and land for building
almshouses. These one-roomed homes stood
along the High Road just south of Scotland
Green for nearly three hundred years, finally
being declared unfit for habitation in 1905.

Alongside the inns and tradesmen's houses
were the mansions of the wealthy local
landowners, set within the walls of their
enclosed gardens. One such was the 'sumptuous

fair house' just north of Scotland Green of Nathaniell Martin, citizen and goldsmith of London. Further down, at the corner where White Hart Lane meets the High Street, was the even larger house of Sir Edward Barkham, bordered on the north and east by the Moselle stream. Barkham's 'mansion house', as it was called, had barns, stables, gardens and an orchard. Sir Edward was a very significant figure in Tottenham who, apart from this house, also possessed several separate parcels of land and a wood eventually becoming Crooks farm, one of the oldest identified farms in Tottenham.

Other major landowners appearing on the map include the heirs to the lands acquired by William Lock and his sons Matthew and Thomas. Lock was a London mercer and alderman who started acquiring lands and tenements in Tottenham from the 1540s. By 1547 he and his sons had acquired around 270 acres of land, groves, houses and other buildings, a substantial amount of which passed to his granddaughter, Elizabeth Candeler (d.1622), and her daughter Lady Ann Heybourne, both of whom continued to live in Tottenham and are commemorated by an impressive monument in All Hallows church.

'THE TENANTS OF THE MANOR HAVE DESPAIRED OF THEIR LIVES'

In contrast with the apparent prosperity and security of the map, the manor rolls reveal that all was not well in relations between the prosperous incomers and the now largely landless labourers and servants. In 1531, for example, John Tyler and his wife caused outrage because they had 'harboured and associated with divers suspected persons so that the tenants of the manor have

37 *The Heybourne tomb, showing Sir Ferdinando Heybourne and his wife Anne (née Candeler), another of the wealthy Locke daughters.*

despaired of their lives'. They were ordered out of the lordship, together with William Martyn and his wife ('a common scold and inciter of the neighbours servants to steal from their masters') and Thomas Edwards, hedgebreaker and thief.

As well as theft, quarrels, hedgebreaking and the trafficking of stolen goods, the court records in the 16th century reveal numerous fights and assaults by fists, spades, sticks, knives and swords. These were clearly troubled times and disturbing to the many respectable and prosperous householders in Tottenham. What brought this about? The drastic shift in land ownership, customary and freehold land being brought up by wealthy London citizens and common land being enclosed, was obviously a strong factor. The change created an increasing population with little, if any, land of its own to farm, or common land for cattle grazing, or woodland for fuel and forage for pigs. A particular loss was the freely available wood and underbrush for cooking and winter warmth, leading to many cases of hedgebreaking. The social distress was not confined to Tottenham, as the pattern was repeated across the country following the Tudor developments in industry and commerce. The Poor Laws were introduced, with the first Overseers of the Poor, attached to the Church Vestry, established to administer some measure of relief.

Another factor particularly affecting Tottenham was a consequence of increased traffic along the High Road and around the parish. We can detect this in the court records. Robert Downes was accused of 'lodging and receiving suspected persons, both men and women, who are not of good fame and rule', whilst the wife of John Wolles 'harboured men who are not of good fame and rule and ordered not to do so any more and not keep an alehouse'. The main highway, as well as drawing in respectable citizens of London who bought their houses and gardens in Tottenham, also brought with them a less desirable class of incomer who mixed with the increasing numbers of landless poor now resident in the village. Into this mix came the travellers passing to and from London, many on legitimate business, but others whose purpose was less respectable and who were moved on as soon as possible.

At the close of the Tudor period Tottenham was more divided by wealth than ever before, increasingly populated by incomers and influenced by the commercial growth of the City of London.

FIVE

The Coleraine Years

In 1626 Hugh Hare (1606-67), 1st Lord Coleraine, purchased the manors of Tottenham, although his main residence was Longford in Wiltshire, and he also owned a house in nearby Totteridge. Coleraine, a young man of 21, had recently risen in the ranks of the aristocracy. He became an intimate of the young King Charles I, and probably spent little time in Tottenham and no time at all in Ireland, in spite of being an Irish baron. But Tottenham's easy access to London meant the Coleraine family remained lords of the manor until the end of the 18th century with an unorthodox female heir. During this time the family played a significant role in the life of the village and saw its progression from an aristocratic manor to one with a vibrant intellectual life and ever closer ties with London's commercial and professional elite.

A VICAR OF DISTINCTION

One of Coleraine's nearest neighbours was a man of remarkable intellect and considerable renown. William Bedwell (1563-1632), the vicar of the parish church of All Hallows, is credited with writing one of the first local histories, *A Brief Description of the Town of Tottenham High Crosse*, published in 1631. Based on ancient manuscripts, the book describes aspects of Tottenham in the 17th century, as well as the historical origins of features such as the name Tottenham (Saxon he thought), the Seven Sisters trees, High Cross and local wells, as well as the likely route of 'the main road from Scotland to London', as he described the High Road.

Bedwell was born in Essex and educated at Cambridge, becoming the vicar of Tottenham in 1607, where he lived for the rest of his life. He was a mathematician and a notable Arabist, with a reputation well beyond his small parish. A fluent knowledge of Arabic contributed to his study of mathematics, where Arabian scholars had primacy, although it was probably in relation to the scriptures that Bedwell was most interested in languages. He became a student of ancient and rabbinic Hebrew, Aramaic and Syriac, and had the distinction of being included on the first committee compiling the new translation of the Bible under King James.

During his early years in Tottenham, Bedwell's reputation was at its height, and he received many international visitors eager to extend their knowledge of Arabic, but he did not travel far from his parish. He seemed happy to settle here with his wife and four daughters. He made just one visit to Europe, to Leiden in Holland, where the University had many Arabic manuscripts and the best printers of Arabic in northern

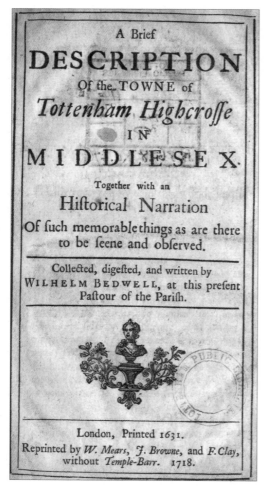

Europe. Bedwell was described as a kind and generous man, but lacking in the drive and assertiveness that would have made his talent and knowledge more widely known. Although he produced some publications in mathematics and Arabic, he never quite achieved his original promise. However, he did write a book that has proved important to local historians and was a stimulus for the 2nd and 3rd Lord Coleraines to write their own history of the parish.

WEALTHY NEIGHBOURS

Coleraine's neighbours in Tottenham were of a similar wealth and standing, and the Hearth Tax of 1664 provides evidence of a number of large mansions in the area. One occasional neighbour was Sir John Coke (c.1563-1648), a Secretary of State who stayed in George Henningham's old home, the Black House in the High Road, during the summer months to avoid the plague and other diseases then rife in London.

To the west, standing on higher ground along White Hart Lane, was the grand Parsonage mentioned in the previous chapter. According to the 18th-century historians Oldfield and Dyson, this house was rebuilt in the 1630s for a Lord of the Admiralty named Soames, using locally made brick, and acquired a moat and drawbridge for added status. The Parsonage, part of the demesne of the Dean and Chapter of St Paul, was thought to be on the site of the old Pembroke manor house. This house, with its moat and extensive

38 *Coat of arms of Hugh Hare, 1st Baron Coleraine, who was made a baron by Charles I in 1625. This coat of arms is carved on to the back of Bruce Castle. Photograph by Henry Jacobs.*

39 *Title page of* A Brief Description of the Town of Tottenham High Crosse, *William Bedwell's history of Tottenham 1631, said to be one of the first local histories to be published.*

grounds, survived into the 20th century and later became known as the Rectory or Moated House, and finally Tottenham Park. It is now the site of the Garden of Peace, the lovely, tranquil part of Tottenham Cemetery.

Other wealthy neighbours were the Barkham family, living in 1619 in a 'fine mansion house' on the east side of Tottenham Green. They owned a considerable amount of land in the parish, including Crooks Farm in White Hart Lane. Sir Edward Barkham was an Alderman and Lord Mayor of London, married to Joan Crouch, an aunt of Coleraine. Sir Edward's eldest sons Edward and Robert also later had houses and land in Tottenham and played a significant part in the life of the parish.

Another house on Tottenham Green was the large mansion of Sir Abraham Reynardson (1590-1661). Reynardson was a very wealthy City merchant and a leading member of the Merchant Taylor Company. He was also a judge of 'Oyer and Terminer', a commission instructed to investigate treason, felony and misdemeanours. In 1648 he reluctantly became the Mayor of London, an unfortunate time to hold a great office. The following years were not kind to Reynardson, Coke and Coleraine.

A NATION DIVIDED

By 1640 King Charles I was beset by problems largely of his own making. Parliament had not met for 11 years and the King was unable to raise money to fight the rebellion in Scotland. By 1642 the antagonism between King and Parliaments came to a head and the Civil War began. The country was divided, and although London was largely Parliamentarian, there were a few Royalists among the City merchants, a division also reflected in Tottenham.

Many, such as the Barkham family, supported Parliament. Sir Edward Barkham, a magistrate from 1645, was a Commissioner for Taxation in Middlesex, and appointed under the Act of 1649 to make assessments on wealthy families to raise money for Parliament. Lady Barkham contributed voluntarily, but other inhabitants were more strongly opposed to what they saw as an unfair tax. Lord Coleraine, a Royalist although his wife was the sister of the Parliamentarian Earl of Manchester, was away in the service of the King when his castle at Longford was seized by Parliamentary forces. His house in Totteridge was also seized, and when these properties were returned after the Restoration they were in a severe state of disrepair. Bruce Castle also suffered neglect during this time. In addition, Coleraine was forced to pay a capital levy to Parliament on his estate in Tottenham, calculated at £2,000. Because he was absent this was raised to £4,000, only reducing when he agreed to return to Bruce Castle.

Sir John Coke and Abraham Reynardson were particularly badly affected by the war. During 1642-3 Reynardson refused to raise loans for Parliament except under compulsion, and in 1648-9, when he was Lord Mayor, he defied Parliament by refusing to proclaim the abolition of the monarchy in London. He declared that his various oaths of office prevented him doing so, but Parliament went ahead with the proclamation, stripped Reynardson of his mayoralty, fined him £2,000 and imprisoned him in the Tower. He refused to pay the fine and his goods and holdings in the East India Company were sold and the proceeds distributed to the poor of London. Reynardson later maintained that he lost some £20,000 as a result of his loyalty to the King, and his reward of a knighthood after the Restoration was not therefore particularly generous. Reynardson returned to Tottenham after his tumultuous experience, and lived quietly with his family until his death in 1661.

Sir John Coke was an elderly man when the Civil War broke out, and at first he supported Parliament but later changed his mind. His

family thought he was unsafe in his house in Derbyshire, and at the age of 81 he moved back to Tottenham, where he was assessed by Parliament for £1,000. He refused to pay, but died in 1644 before the warrant ordering payment could be carried out.

THE CHANGING PARISH

Following the upheavals of the Civil War, a dynamic, confident group of people representing London's growing professional class began to take up residence in Tottenham, influencing education, social reform and parish affairs. The most significant members of this

40   *(Left) Sir John Coke, Secretary of State to Charles I, resident of the Black House in Tottenham, where he died during the Civil War.*

42 *Sir Abraham Reynardson's house on Tottenham Green. Reynardson, a wealthy London merchant, was Lord Mayor in 1648, when he found himself in opposition to Parliament over the proposed beheading of Charles I.*

group were the Quakers, and a Tottenham Friends Meeting was already established here when national founder George Fox visited in 1689. The Friends continued to thrive in Tottenham throughout the 18th and 19th centuries, and after a period meeting in hired premises land was purchased for a building on the High Road in 1714. The building was enlarged in 1777, and later the orchard behind the Meeting House was bought and used as a burial ground, the first burial in 1802 being that of Thomas Gorman, age seven.

41 *(Left) The Rectory House, White Hart Lane, formerly the Parsonage, on Rectory Manor land. It was rebuilt during the 1630s by a Lord of the Admiralty, and was one of the largest houses in the parish.*

Tottenham Friends were prominent in social reform and education. Josiah Forster (1693-1763) moved to Tottenham in 1751 to open a school in Reynardson's old house on the Green, and his family were at the forefront of many local and national actions. His son William (1747-1824), a schoolmaster and surveyor, was active in parish affairs, becoming a churchwarden and attempting to bring order and humanity to the condition of the poor in the local workhouse. Tottenham Quakers were also engaged in the campaign against the slave trade and led by William Dilwyn (1743-1824,) who brought the movement to England from the American Quakers in the 1770s. Later in the 19th century, Josiah's grandsons William, Josiah and Robert continued the campaign against slavery in America and those countries still trading in human bondage. William, born in 1784, was a Quaker minister of considerable oratory and intellect who was engaged in many areas of social reform. He visited London prisons in 1813 and reported back to Elizabeth Fry on

43 *The Quaker Meeting House was built in 1714 and is shown here in 1909. A cemetery was added behind the building in 1802.*

the appalling conditions for women in Newgate, and in later years worked for famine relief in blight-stricken Ireland. Towards the end of his life Forster became more active in the anti-slavery campaign, travelling to America, and it was in America in 1854 that he died.

Another significant Quaker social reformer and anti-slavery campaigner was Priscilla Wakefield (1750-1832), an aunt of Elizabeth Fry. Priscilla established a lying-in charity in 1791 to help poor women in pregnancy with linen and a small amount of money. In 1798 she set up a Benefit Club, which she ran from her home in the Old Ship Yard, High Cross, to encourage poor women and children to save. This prototype of the Savings Bank moved to the grammar school on a more formal footing and was later extended to include labourers. Priscilla was also very interested in education, particularly for girls, and was instrumental in establishing the Green Coat school in 1792. She was also a prolific writer of educational books for children, and this is how she made her living.

44 *Priscilla Wakefield, local Quaker, philanthropist and author of children's books, set up a prototype of the first savings bank, and was instrumental in building the Greencoat school.*

Several members of the Forster family lived in Philip Lane, where in 1862 they conveyed four newly built cottages to a trust of members of the Tottenham Meeting. The houses were to be maintained by the trustees, who would choose the residents from Tottenham people, not necessarily Quakers but preferably widows or spinsters aged at least fifty-five; the houses still stand today. Several other Quaker families lived in the large houses in Bruce Grove, and the most notable of these was Luke Howard (1772-1864), who lived at No. 7. Howard was a partner in a chemical firm in Plaistow, and then ran his own manufacturing laboratory in Stratford by 1807. Both concerns were successful and he was a wealthy man, but it is his interest in meteorology that brought him most fame through his classification of the different types of clouds and the foundation of meteorology as a science.

SCHOOLS FOR THE POOR

Tottenham's affluent population was undoubtedly well educated, but for those who could not afford private education there were few opportunities to acquire even the basic skills. There was probably a village school from the 16th century as there is a mention of a schoolmaster, Anthony Dale, in the parish records. But it was not until the endowment made to Tottenham Grammar School by Sarah, Duchess of Somerset (1631-92)

45 *(Above) Luke Howard, Quaker and a pioneer in meteorology, lived at No. 7 Bruce Grove. The building is still standing today, but in a very dilapidated condition.*

46 *(Left) Sarah, Duchess of Somerset was the wife of the 2nd Lord Coleraine. She endowed the local grammar school in her will, enabling it to be rebuilt and a teacher to be employed on a regular basis.*

47   *The grammar school in the High Road, c.1900.*

and wife of the 2nd Lord Coleraine, that the school can be firmly established in history. Her will of 1686 provided for a new school building, with additional money for maintenance and salaries for the schoolmaster and an usher. By the early part of the 18th century the grammar school was securely established, with the help of additional charity bequests.

In the High Road, just north of High Cross, the school provided for up to 80 boys between the ages of 7 and 14, and taught reading, handwriting, grammar and basic arithmetic, as well as the catechism. Boys from the parish could only be admitted with a certificate from the school's trustees, and an undertaking from their parents that they would keep their children free from vermin and sent to school clean and decent.

Girls' education was provided for with the establishment of two charity schools in the 18th century, largely supported by voluntary subscription. The Blue Coat school was opened in 1735 and took up to forty girls between the age of 7 and 14. They were taught reading, writing, knitting, needlework and a 'little arithmetic'. The girls were nominated by subscribers and given a blue uniform and expected to attend the parish church. The school on Scotland Green, rebuilt in 1833 and enlarged in 1876, still stands today, having undergone many changes of use and modifications.

The School of Industry, more usually known as the Green Coat school from the uniform provided, was opened in 1792 in the High Road by Stoneley South, and provided the same curriculum for up to forty girls. It transferred to a new building behind the grammar school in Somerset Road in 1863, where it continues today as the Green School. It was established largely through the efforts of Priscilla Wakefield, with the support of voluntary subscribers and income from the girls work, and, like the Blue Coat school, was closely connected to the local church, Holy Trinity.

THE LAST COLERAINES

Henry Hare (1635-1708), 2nd Baron Coleraine, inherited his title from his father in 1667, and was something of an antiquarian and architect. This led him to follow Bedwell's example and write his own unpublished history of Tottenham, *The History and Antiquities of the Town and Church of Tottenham in Middlesex*, dated 1715. This interest in the past and in Bedwell's work probably influenced his remodelling of Bruce Castle, still known as the Lordship House, during the 1680s and his involvement in work on the church, he also

provided for the maintenance of local ancient features such as the elm trees at Page Green, known as the Seven Sisters.

Coleraine had sold his house in Totteridge by the 1680s and Tottenham became his London residence and particularly important as he was a fairly active Member of Parliament for Old Sarum. Bruce Castle had been neglected during the Civil War and hardly touched for a century but Coleraine had it renovated, probably to his own design. The original east and west ends were demolished and rebuilt and the distinctive two-storey porch with the clock tower was added. He also retained the old brick tower, 'in respective of its great antiquity more than conveniency', although he had to confess he did not know its real purpose. His antiquarian – one might say romantic – interest also extended to the church. He instructed the workmen in 1690 to pin back the roots of the ivy torn from the tower to increase its picturesque effect. He also paid for a vestry

48 *The Bluecoat school on Scotland Green after rebuilding in 1833. The building, much renovated and extended, can still be seen today, now extended for housing.*

49 *Henry Hare, 2nd Lord Coleraine, inherited the manor in 1667 and made Bruce Castle his main London residence.*

and mausoleum to be built on the east end of the church, probably commissioning Nicholas Hawksmoor for the task. The vestry was demolished in 1875 as a result of Butterfield's unfortunate renovations.

Coleraine's history was revised by his grandson, also Henry Hare (1693-1749), who was a keen antiquarian. Hare became the 3rd Baron Coleraine in 1708, age 15, following the death of his grandfather, his father having died a year earlier. His childless marriage to the wealthy Anne Hanger in 1720 was unhappy from the start, and she left him two years later. This allowed Henry to pursue his intellectual leanings, including collecting paintings, coins and medals, as well as a number of antiquities, mainly bought on his European tours. Henry meanwhile sold Longford in 1717 and made Bruce Castle his home, making further renovations in keeping with a fashionable house of the day.

50 *A 1686 painting of Bruce Castle, showing the renovations to his own designs by the 2nd Lord Coleraine. The house had been neglected during the Civil War period.*

51 *Engraving of Tottenham parish church by Henrietta Townsend, showing Lord Coleraine's mausoleum.*

52 *James Townsend, who became lord of the manor as a trustee of Henrietta Townsend (his wife). Henrietta had been named heir in Coleraine's will but was unable to claim her rights as she had been born in Italy.*

It was on one of his tours that his illegitimate daughter, Henrietta Rosa Peregrina, was born in Italy in 1745. Coleraine and Henrietta's mother, Rose Duplessis, the daughter of a French clergyman, had entered into 'a solemn, mutual engagement to take each other for husband and wife'. Unfortunately Coleraine died shortly after Henrietta's birth, and although he attempted to leave his estates to her there was a challenge on the basis that she was foreign-born.

HENRIETTA ROSA TOWNSEND

Henrietta had originally been recognised as the lady of the manors, but as an alien her right was challenged, although Coleraine's other heirs were excluded at the same time because of the terms of his will. The manors and lands therefore escheated to the Crown. It can be imagined that Rosa Duplessis fought strongly for her daughter's rights, and eventually

53   *Modern day Bruce Castle showing some of the modifications and renovations carried out in the 17th and 18th centuries.*

Henrietta did return to Bruce Castle as the lady of the manor. Through a private Act of Parliament, the MP Chauncey Townsend achieved the grant of the manors to Henrietta's trustees, and, as she had by this time married Townsend's son James when she was 18, he became one of these trustees. The Tottenham estates and manors came to the Townsend family, and the title of Baron Coleraine went to a more distant relative.

Henrietta was an artist and left several fine engravings of Tottenham which complement the local history written by her father and great grandfather. Many were used to illustrate the later, and more comprehensive, 19th-century history of Tottenham written by William Robinson.

Henrietta's son, Henry Hare Townsend, somewhat strapped for cash, did not share this interest in the manors. The Coleraine family ceased their association with Tottenham in 1789, when Bruce Castle and most of the lands were auctioned, followed in 1792 by the sale of the lordships to Thomas Smith. Smith briefly held the manors and Bruce Castle but in 1805 they were sold to Sir William Curtis, and thereafter they descended in the Curtis family. Meanwhile, Bruce Castle, now separated from the manors went on to have a varied and interesting history in its own right.

SIX

Managing Change

With its growing population of incomers of every social standing, Tottenham by the mid-18th century needed new ways of managing social relationships and in particular meeting the needs of the very poorest in the community. The once vigorous manor courts continued to meet throughout the 19th century, usually at the *Plough Inn*, but now gave way to the Parish Vestry, named after the church vestry where it originally met. Actively encouraged by Parliament through various Acts passed from the 16th century onwards, the Vestry progressively widened its remit to include the collection of the Poor Rate as well as Church Rate, the election of parish officers, and overseeing the relief of the poor. It also decided on local issues including highways, policing, health and decisions relating to the remaining common land.

PARISH OFFICERS

The most important Vestry meeting was at Easter, when parish officials, usually unpaid, were elected from names nominated by the wards. The few officers that were paid included the vestry clerk, the sexton and the beadle, but others, such as the churchwardens and the overseers, were not salaried. Tottenham was divided into four wards from the 16th century.

The Nether (later Lower), Middle and High Cross wards, running north to south and eastwards to the river Lea, accounted for roughly half of the acreage. The less densely populated Wood Green ward, which went roughly from the Moselle and High Road to Tottenham's western boundary, covered the rest.

The important post of churchwarden, originally largely ecclesiastical, became increasingly engaged in civil matters in the parish. From 1776 two churchwardens were chosen at Easter, one elected by the inhabitants and the other by the vicar. The churchwardens were answerable to the bishop, and were responsible for the maintenance of the church building. They were also required to report annually on the moral state of the parish and were involved in the relief of the poor. Not everyone had the time or inclination to fulfil the duties of this post, but reasons for exemption were few unless a fine – £10 in 1733 – was paid. In 1743 John Bell refused to serve on the not unreasonable grounds that he was a Protestant dissenter, but the Vestry insisted this was not a reason for exemption. Later in the century, the Quaker William Forster (1784-1854) chose to hold the position as part of his active work in the local community, even though the post was partly ecclesiastical.

54   *The* Old Plough Inn, *c.1880. Manor courts were still held here as late as 1870, although by then the parish was largely administered by the Vestry and the Board of Health.*

To the Inhabitants of the Parish of Tottenham.

LADIES AND GENTLEMEN,

The Office of BEADLE having become vacant by your appointment of JOSEPH FORSTER to that of SEXTON, I beg most respectfully to offer myself to your notice, as a Candidate for the

OFFICE OF BEADLE

having been Street Keeper and Constable, more than ten years, which Office I trust I should have had the honor to have retained, had not the operations of the New Poor Law abolished it.

As a claim upon your sympathies, permit me to state, that I have a Family of seven Children, and a Wife who has been afflicted for some years past, depending on my very casual resources.

I am,

Ladies and Gentlemen,

Your obedient humble Servant,

JOHN FOWLER

CHURCH ROAD,
Tottenham, July 4th, 1838.

55   *John Fowler elicits the sympathy vote, as well as putting forward his credentials for the post of beadle in 1838.*

COLLECTING THE RATES

The overseers of the poor were chosen at Easter, two for each ward for a two-year period. This was a particularly unpopular post as the holders were required to collect the Poor Rate set four times a year by the Vestry and be responsible for giving relief to the destitute poor. The Poor Rate was levied on any house with a rentable value of £5 or more a year, and was paid in addition to the Church Rate. The amount of this rate rose steadily, from £763 in 1775-6 to a peak of £4,065 in 1821. In 1756 the Vestry decided to support the overseers with the appointment of an assistant with powers in all four wards. His main task was to remove vagrants from the parish to ensure they did not become a burden on the rates. The Vestry appointed a paid official to the post in 1819 following an Act of Parliament that permitted salaried overseers.

The destitute in Tottenham – those unable to work and with no other means of support – were helped out in a number of ways, few of which were adequate or without harshness. Some received a small pension, and others food, fuel or clothing, but such casual handouts were discouraged and many people became subject to the new regime brought in during the 18th century of indoor relief provided by the workhouse.

'PLAN FOR THE FUTURE MANAGEMENT OF THE POOR'

The workhouse – the institution that came to symbolise so much in relation to deprivation, humiliation and pain over the course of the 19th century – was introduced at the beginning of the 18th century when a Parliamentary Act gave parishes authority to buy or rent a building and enter into contracts with businessmen to house, maintain and employ parish paupers.

Tottenham Vestry decided to open a parish workhouse in 1725, but the establishment had

56 *Coombes Croft House, c.1920. Originally built as the parish workhouse around 1760, it later became a school and then an orphanage, and was eventually used by Tottenham Urban District Council for various offices, including a library.*

a varied and erratic history. Ever anxious to meet basic needs at minimal cost, the Vestry oscillated between running its own workhouse and contracting out. In 1747, for instance, the workhouse committee decided they would get better value by contracting with Mr Thruckstone to take care of the poor in his house in West Green. This was a surprising choice, as the committee must have been aware there had been concerns when Thruckstone housed the poor from another parish and the Vestry was compelled to complain that he brought 'such large quantities of dead bodies' to the cemetery that there was no room for local parishioners. Later the contract went to Samuel Tull, until again there were reports of ill-treatment. Despite such problems, the Vestry frequently resorted to farming out their poor.

When the poor of the village were not being contracted out to businessmen, they were housed in the parish workhouse under direct management of the Vestry. The first workhouse was a rented building, and it was not until the 1760s that the parish built its own workhouse, on the Coombes Croft charity land in Marsh Lane. Forty-four inmates were recorded there in 1765-6, but numbers continued to grow and an additional wing was added in 1813. By the time the workhouse was closed, in 1837, there were 150 paupers. Coombes Croft, as the workhouse was called, went on to have a varied history. After periods as a boarding school, orphanage and laundry, it was used for municipal purposes by 1872, becoming at times offices for the Board of Health, the Education Committee, and libraries.

Management of the workhouse was not always satisfactory, and in 1789 the Vestry met to consider a Plan for the Management of the Poor, establishing a committee of 24 guardians and regulations for the general conduct of the workhouse. The committee met monthly at the workhouse and four members carried out weekly inspections, whilst 'suitable' ladies gave out advice to the women. The regulations and committee visits were intended to ensure a more efficient and well-ordered workhouse. The Quaker William Forster appears to have been a leading force behind this Plan, as this is the time when he became churchwarden. He followed this up in 1793, when a team investigated the conditions, and in 1791 he accompanied the Rev. Mr Hardy to the worsted factory in Cuckney, Nottinghamshire where a number of Tottenham pauper children had been sent as apprentices. Finding that the

57 *The* Bell and Hare Tavern, *c.1890, by Park Lane, built on the Charity Estate land and originally called* The Three Conies.

58   *The Pheasaunts almshouses were originally built alongside the church in the 16th century, but were rebuilt on this spot by the Pound in 1744 and then renamed the Pound Almshouses.*

children appeared 'healthy and content with their situation', it was recommended that the practice continue.

The 1789 regulations set out an exacting regime. All the inmates – they were termed 'the family' – had to rise at seven in the winter and six in the summer. After washing and breakfast the adults reported to the workroom for a full day's work. Bedtime for all was eight in the winter and nine in the summer. The family had to do daily sweeping and a thorough cleaning of the house once a week, a task usually allocated to the girls. They were taken to church twice on Sundays and on Wednesday mornings, with bible readings after supper. None of the inmates were allowed out without permission, but they were allowed to keep 2d. in the shilling of the money they earned. A few concessions were made for the old or infirm, and some allowance made for the children. They also had to report to the workroom soon after rising, having 'washed

and combed without loss of time', but were also allowed an hour for breakfast and play in the mornings and one and a half hours for dinner. Children were to be taught to read, and the regime clearly became more progressive following Forster's initiatives.

Diet in the workhouse was frugal, and Tottenham introduced the cheaper pork, instead of beef or mutton, well before other parishes such as Edmonton. Whilst costs were kept to a minimum, the income was maximised from the work of the inmates. The treasurer's accounts for 1737, for instance, show that £23 9s. 3d. was received from silk-winding done by the children alone. Set against that was the 16s. 6d. spent on sixty pounds of pork and 12s. on three bushels of oatmeal. In spite of this, the cost of the poor continued to rise. Inefficiency, lax monitoring of accounts and exploitation of the system by masters and businessmen undoubtedly contributed to the increased costs, although there must also have been an actual rise in the numbers of local destitute.

The parish did its best to prevent people coming to the village who might become a burden on the rates, and even those with settled employment had to produce certificates showing their parish of residence. But it was difficult in a place like Tottenham, so close to the city and on a main road, to keep people out. As industrialisation and demand for a more flexible workforce grew, periodic and chronic unemployment became a national problem, and Parliament responded with the Act of 1837 which organised workhouses across a larger area. Tottenham joined with Edmonton, Enfield, Hampstead, Hornsey, Cheshunt and Waltham Abbey in the Edmonton Poor Law Union of 1837, and the Tottenham workhouse closed, its inmates dispersed to different workhouses outside the parish and families split up by age and gender.

59 *Reynardson's Almshouses, with the central chapel, were opened in 1737 on the High Road near the grammar school, and finally closed in 1938.*

CHARITY OUTSIDE THE WORKHOUSE

Clothing, food and small payments had long been given to the needy by the churchwardens at the vicar's direction, including charity bequests to the poor. Much of this charity money had become part of the parish income, as well as income from the common, and was used to supplement the poor rate. But support given in this way, outside the workhouse, usually known as out-relief, was objected to by those who believed the poor should be made to work for their benefits and kept in a more orderly environment. Charitable bequests by residents such as Balthazar Sanchez, Lady Coleraine, Sir Robert Barkham and Jane Barkham, among others, had left money or pieces of land to provide income to be distributed among the poor as food, fuel, clothing or pensions. These charities depended on the honesty and efficiency of the trustees to ensure they were effectively maintained and administered over the following generations but, not surprisingly, this was not always the case. As early as William Bedwell's time in 1631 the neglect of charities was noted.

Many came to be administered by the church, and eventually the Vestry, and were treated as common parish property. One group of charities was put together in 1634 into the Charity Estates, and were vested in the vicar and other trustees to administer for the benefits of the poor. The money was used for the purchase of a house near White Hart Lane, some land

at Combes Croft (later used for the workhouse) and the Pond field at Downhills. The White Hart Lane house, called *The Three Conies* in 1725, had become *The Bell and Hare* inn by 1825.

THE OLD AND INFIRM

Elderly people no longer fit for work had long been accepted as deserving of charitable support. Almshouses – usually no more than one room – were first referred to in the 14th century, and by the 18th century there were three such establishments. The oldest, known as Pheasaunts, was founded in the 16th century by George Henningham (d.1536), whose daughter married Jasper Pheasaunt. These homes for three poor widows were built alongside the church, but by the 18th century they were clearly causing distress to respectable churchgoers. Lord Coleraine complained in his history 'of an horrible abuse that is a detriment to God's service and the church's cleanliness, for it is a great desecration of a church to have nastiness near it (at the very threshold).' The complaint, it appears, referred to one of the tenements being used for brewing beer. Eventually these houses were demolished and by 1744 were replaced by new ones next to the parish pound in the High Road. The accommodation for three was increased to seven in 1847 and the two sets of homes were known as the Old and New Pound almshouses. By 1893 the accommodation was considered cramped and inconvenient and by 1925, when residents had voted with their feet and left, the sale of the almshouses was sanctioned.

The Sanchez almshouses were built by the Spaniard Balthazar Sanchez in 1600 for eight men and women. These single-roomed brick-built homes were erected along the High Road just south of Scotland Green. Over the years various renovations were carried out according to the terms of the will, but by 1825 they were regarded as barely habitable due to damp caused by being below the level of the High Road. By 1868 a complete rebuilding was being urged, but it never took place and by 1919 the sale of the almshouses was sanctioned. Six years later the buildings were demolished to make way for Burgess' Department Store.

Reynardson's almshouses were opened in 1737 next to the grammar school and were built and maintained by money left by Sir Nicholas Reynardson in his will of 1685. The eight two-storey apartments had a central chapel to provide for daily prayers and the instruction of 20 poor children, although the children's instruction seems not to have taken place, and

60 *This picture by Hunnings, the photographers, shows Mr Fowler, the beadle c.1870. Fowler was the last person to hold this office.*

the daily prayers had become weekly by 1851. By 1825 the homes were in poor repair and work was carried out, and sixty years later they were still thought satisfactory. In 1938 the sale of the almshouses was authorised when the last two residents moved to Draper's almshouses in Bruce Grove.

'VERY DANGEROUS IN THE WINTER'

The posts of constable and beadle, once elected by the manor courts, had by the mid-18th century come under the Vestry, and the period saw the gradual introduction of a police force and better lit streets. Constables, appointed one for each ward, were the principal officers responsible for law and order in the parish. They had to be presented to the local Justice of the Peace for approval, and on the rare occasion when this was not given the appointment was referred back to the court baron of the manor. Assisting the constable in keeping the parish in an orderly state was the beadle. Beadles appear to have been men of working-class background who were paid a salary of £10 in the mid-18th century, rising to £40 by 1810. The beadle was required to walk at least daily around the principal part of the parish and deal with vagrants and any other people causing difficulty. He had also to check lodging houses for any suspicious person who might become chargeable to the parish, and visit public houses and report on any misconduct. Not surprisingly, the beadle was expected to be respectful to inhabitants and be steady, sober and orderly – and not to swear. At all events, he was to preserve the peace and prevent unnecessary expense. At one point during the middle of the 18th century the post was combined with that of assistant workhouse master, and in 1794 the Vestry decided he should hold an official appointment as assistant constable.

Other moves were made periodically to support safety in the parish, including a parish

61   *Dick Turpin, the most notorious of the highwaymen who threatened travellers in the locality. Turpin was said to ride local streets, including Hanger Lane.*

cage in 1743, replaced by a watchhouse in 1800 on Scotland Green. In 1774 the Vestry raised a special rate for the trustees of the Stamford Hill Turnpike Trust to light and watch the High Road during the winter months, when the darkness hid all sorts of perils. The High Road, according to a 1774 petition to Parliament, was 'very dangerous in the winter season, being often in the night time infested with robbers'.

The early 19th century, however, was a period of occasional intervention and back-pedalling. A watchhouse keeper was employed only from 1821-7, and in 1833 the Vestry adopted the Lighting and Watching Act but failed to reappoint inspectors after three years and a temporary constable had to be provided by private subscribers. The Vestry declined to seek the introduction of the New Police in 1830, or to take over the watching of turnpike roads. By 1840, however, it was clear more regular strategies needed to be put in place. Tottenham achieved inclusion within the Metropolitan Police area and in 1841 adopted the Turnpike

Lighting Act and appointed lighting inspectors. Under the Metropolitan Police, 13 constables and two sergeants patrolled the area.

CHOLERA AND CLEAN WATER

Until the turn of the 19th century, sickness and health was addressed at an individual level. Those who could afford it paid for medical help. There had been occasional payments for medical services to the poor since the 17th century, a Vestry-appointed physician being paid a retainer and fees, but by the 19th century an increasing number of health issues affected the whole community in one way or another thanks to a steadily increasing population, overcrowded houses, inadequate sewerage and an equally inadequate water supply. Residents complained to the Vestry that there was no good water supply in the village, and they had to pay water carriers to fetch it from the well in Tottenham Green. By 1840 further wells had been sunk at Page Green and Tottenham Hale, as well as one opened by the Vestry opposite the *Bell and Hare*.

The biggest jolt to public awareness came with the cholera outbreaks of 1831 and 1832. Albert Hill, a pupil at Bruce Castle school, remembers being kept in isolation, pupils and staff being forbidden to go into the village for several weeks. When cholera was reported nearby in March 1832, consideration was given to converting the *Bell and Hare* into an infirmary for patients, but it was too near the workhouse for safety. In the event, there was a comparatively low death toll of some 20 people, mostly paupers from the workhouse.

It was this event that prompted local inhabitants to set up a provisional Board of Health in December 1831, chaired by Edwin

62 *The pump and well at Tottenham High Cross, painted by Russell Bell in 1908. Many residents had to get their water from wells such as this. Some of them paid water carriers to fetch it for them.*

To the Ratepayers of Tottenham.

TOTTENHAM, FEB. 28, 1872.

On behalf of myself and others, I beg to
request the favour of your Nomination of
the following Gentlemen as Candidates for
the Membership of the Local Board of
Health at the forthcoming Election:

ROBERT LUKE HOWARD, Civil Engineer
THOMAS BISCOE, Gentleman
RALPH LITTLER, Barrister at Law
JOSHUA PEDLEY, Solicitor

Yours faithfully,

ALBERT HILL.

Please send the Nomination Paper to
Mr. W. Hall, Tottenham, BEFORE March
6th.

63   *Campaign leaflet to Tottenham Ratepayers for
the permanent Board of Health that succeeded the
one established in 1831.*

Hill (1793-1876), Albert's father. A survey of the
parish was produced, identifying the main trouble
spots. There was dung in householder's yards,
blood and offal uncollected in slaughterhouses,
and ditches at the back of buildings in a
lamentable condition. The common sewers were
in a poor state, especially Carbuncle Ditch
formerly Garbell Ditch, branching off from
the Moselle at Scotland Green. Landlords and
tenants were required to take action, and the
Moselle was cleaned and deepened with the use
of pauper labour. It was optimistically claimed
that, with the co-operation of the inhabitants,
most of the nuisances had been dealt with by
the following August.

At the end of March 1832 the Privy Council
made the temporary Board of Health official,
with powers to provide short-term hospitals
for cholera cases, assist the poor in their own
homes with medicine and nursing when they
could not go to hospital, whitewash and
clean houses, remove corrupt and offensive
matter, and destroy clothing and bedding from
infected cases. Medical inspectors would also
visit lodging houses daily and inspect 'tramps
and vagrants'. In September Mr Hill asked
the Vestry to recognise the Board formally,
and this was agreed, with the inclusion of
six Vestry members on the committee. The
alarm engendered by the cholera outbreak
led to the formation of the first of the *ad hoc*
boards and committees that were gradually to
take over the work of the Vestry during the
19th century and lead to the formation of
local government.

SEVEN

Masters, Mistresses and Boarding Schools

A particularly interesting feature of Tottenham was the number of boarding schools established here, catering largely for middle-class families looking for alternatives to the traditional grammar schools. As early as the late 17th century, two renowned educationalists, Mark Lewis (1621-81) and Bathsua Makin (1600-75), opened schools in Tottenham. Makin, one of the most intelligent and learned women of her time, established 'a school for gentlewomen' at Tottenham High Cross in the 1670s. Bathsua Makin, who had tutored Princess Elizabeth, daughter of Charles I, was herself widely educated and determined other women would have the same opportunity. Her prospectus advocated practical, intellectual and moral training, and included grammar, rhetoric, logic, languages, mathematics, geography, history, music, painting and poetry, an exceptionally wide curriculum for any age.

DISSENTING EDUCATION

One group of people which sought a wider education, particularly in scientific and technical subjects, was the Quakers, and they established a number of schools in the parish. It is estimated there had been at least four Quaker schools before 1775, including the boys' school opened by Richard Claridge in 1707 and providing for 20 boarders and a few day pupils. Claridge's principles brought him into conflict with the local establishment, who regarded him as spreading 'heretical and erroneous' opinions. This was not helped by Claridge taking some day pupils free, claiming they had been neglected by the local grammar school, and he was roundly denounced by the master and the vicar. Claridge's school was on Tottenham Green and thought to be the residence of Alderman Barkham in 1619. The building adjoined the *Old Ship* inn, located behind the present High Cross Congregational church, and continued as a school under different masters and was renamed 'Sunnyside' in the late 19th century. After being used as a bicycle workshop, it became dilapidated and untenanted. It was pulled down in 1910 as a 'dangerous eyesore'.

The Quaker Josiah Forster (1693-1763) came to Tottenham in 1752 and opened a boarding school in Reynardson's old house on the Green. This large mansion also served as living accommodation for Forster and his family, and the ballroom was apparently used as the schoolroom. Forster's school offered a technical and commercial syllabus, providing the more practical curriculum sought by the professional middle class. After Forster's death in 1763, the school was taken over by his wife Jane and then by his son-in-law, Thomas Coar, and by Josiah Forster from 1810. The school later moved to

Eagle House, on the west side of Tottenham Green, and was run by Deborah and Fanny Coar as a boys' preparatory school. Later in the century Eagle House became a school for mainly foreign students under the headship of Dr Andrew Price, having long since ceased to be a Quaker school.

Eagle House was near the former town hall, and flanked by the more prestigious Quaker boarding school, Grove House, where we nowadays find

64 *(Left) Bathsua Makin (1600-75), writer and educationist, opened a school in Tottenham. She sought to give girls a full and varied education, better even than the one provided for boys at the time.*

65 *(Below) Sunnyside on Tottenham Green in 1907, the former residence of Alderman Barker. Richard Claridge opened a controversial school here in 1707, and it continued to be used as a school until the end of the 19th century.*

66 *The former house on the Green of Sir Abraham Reynardson's was used as the family home and school run by Josiah Forster in 1752, and continued by his wife Jane after his death in 1763.*

the College of North East London. Grove House opened in 1828 and offered an advanced curriculum and an ethos that rejected the use of corporal punishment. The school was founded by Quakers, but the last headmaster, Arthur Abbott, who also became the lessee from 1871, accepted non-Quakers from 1873. Shortly after becoming an Anglican and buying the school in 1877, he abruptly closed it.

Grove House had a long list of distinguished alumni, including Lord Lister (1827-1912), the surgeon who brought greater safety to medical procedures through the introduction of antiseptic procedures, Daniel Tuke, another physician who specialised in mental illness, Sir Robert Fowler, a banker and politician born of a Quaker family in Tottenham, and William Forster. Forster (1818-86) was a social reformer and politician who followed his family's interest in education and in 1870 introduced the Education Act that started the process of free state education for all.

THE SCHOOL IN THE MANOR HOUSE

In 1827 Thomas Wright Hill (1763-1851) purchased the former manor house with its extensive grounds and opened the most distinguished of Tottenham schools, Bruce Castle. Hill moved from Birmingham, where he ran Hazelwood School, and for the first six years continued with both establishments until the Birmingham school was closed. The first headmaster of Bruce Castle was his son, Rowland Hill (1795-1879), and Rowland's brother Edwin (1793-1876) managed the commercial side. Thomas remained in Tottenham, dying in his house in Bruce Terrace, but it was the Hill brothers, especially Rowland and the oldest Matthew, who were particularly responsible for the radical educational thought that informed the syllabus and ethos of Bruce Castle and attracted people such as Jeremy Bentham,

67   *Eagle House on the Green near the former town hall was used as a school by the Quaker Coar family.*

68   *Grove House in 1842, now the site of the College of North East London. Grove House was a nationally renowned Quaker school, with a long list of distinguished alumni, including W.E. Forster, MP, and Lord Lister.*

69 *Back view of Bruce Castle, following alterations made when the former manor house became a school run by the Hill family. The additional wing on the right housed the school rooms downstairs, with the dormitories upstairs.*

Charles Babbage and Charles Dickens. Dickens wrote admiringly of the methods used as 'the only recognition of education as a broad system of moral and intellectual philosophy that I have ever seen in practice'.

The school had a relaxed approach to discipline, with no corporal punishment and a system of tokens as reward for good work. The tokens could be lost for bad behaviour and exchanged for rewards and privileges as a form of currency within the school. Bruce Castle produced its own magazine from 1839 to 1889, printed by the boys on the school machine and providing a wealth of information about the running of the school and leisure activities. The first edition offers an account of a lecture by Michael Faraday and a review of a school theatrical production, indicating a curriculum that embraced arts and science and did not touch on either superficially.

Whilst the school itself had a nationwide reputation, members of the Hill family also achieved considerable fame. The best known is Sir Rowland Hill, who started his career in education at the age of 12, when he became an assistant in his father's first school. He had a restless intelligence that was not satisfied with

teaching, and in 1837 published *Post Office Reform: its Importance and Practicability*, which dealt with ways of reforming the post by changes in the delivery system and the use of prepayment

70 *Rowland Hill, the postal reformer, helped establish Bruce Castle school where he was headteacher, before moving to the Post Office.*

71 *Arthur Hill was headteacher of Bruce Castle school from c.1840 to 1866. Hill lived in the 18th-century Prioryside in Church Lane, now Parkside Preparatory School.*

through stamps. Shortly after publication he became attached to the Treasury, leading to the introduction of the Penny Post system, and in 1846 entered the Post Office as secretary to the Postmaster General.

Edwin followed Hill into the Post Office in 1840. He was particularly interested in mechanical experiments and invented many machines, including one for folding envelopes. The Hills' younger brother, Arthur, became headmaster of Bruce Castle and remained in charge until 1866, when he was succeeded by his son Dr Birkbeck Hill. The school passed out of the hands of the Hill family in 1877 and eventually closed in 1891.

This was a crucial time for the old manor house, but it was saved from inevitable redevelopment by Joshua Pedley (1832-1912), who bought it. Pedley, a local philanthropist and teetotal Baptist, persuaded Tottenham Urban

District Council to purchase the grounds and Tottenham's first public park was opened in 1903. The Council also acquired the building, opening it as a museum in 1906, although it has also served at times as various council offices.

DAY SCHOOLS FOR THE MIDDLE CLASSES

Alongside the boarding schools, an increasing numbers of day schools catered for the middle class during the 19th century. Fourteen private institutions are listed in 1832, rising to 40 in 1880, many occupying the large houses originally built for the wealthy families who had left the district, such as Moselle House in the High Road opposite Park Road. The Cedars, near the Spurs ground, housed one of the largest of the private schools, Tottenham College, which later moved to White Hart Lane on the corner of Selby Road, close to the present Sixth Form Centre. Like many of the other schools, it attracted a large number of foreign students, printing brochures in French, with terms quoted in francs. There were probably many local French people or people of French origin, as Tottenham had attracted French immigrants from the end of the 18th century.

Many of these schools were short-lived, but the well-established Grammar School continued to provide a solid education for boys in its premises in Somerset Road. It experienced a disastrous inspection report in 1865, after which it was reformed and reopened in 1877 as a fee-paying secondary school for middle-class children. In 1869, following the Endowed Schools Act, it joined a network of grammar schools across the country providing secondary education.

After the 1902 Education Act, two more grammar schools were erected by Middlesex County Council. The first, the County School, already in place by 1901, was most unusually a mixed school, and received fierce criticism. It

72   *Draper's College at High Cross, built as a boys' school in 1858, then closed and re-opened as a girls' school in 1885. It later became the County Council High School for Girls.*

73   *Boys from Lancasterian school taking physical exercise in 1910.*

74 *The Hermitage Schools in Hanger Lane in 1860, built largely with the financial support of Fowler Newsam, who also financed the building of St Ann's church. The name of the schools, and the road, were later changed to St Ann's.*

occupied the Grove House building until new premises were built on the east side of Tottenham Green alongside the municipal buildings. In 1909 the MCC took over the running of the private Drapers High School for girls in the High Road. The three grammar schools catered for fee-paying middle-class students, but in 1909 a quarter of the places were free to scholarship children from the elementary schools, enabling brighter working-class children to gain access to secondary education.

EDUCATING THE WORKING CLASS

For those who could not afford to pay for education there was limited provision of schools, funded by voluntary subscribers but still requiring the payment of the school pence. At the turn of the 19th century there was still just the grammar school for boys and the two

girls' charity schools, the Blue and the Green, providing for some 140 children altogether. These barely kept pace with the increase in population, which by 1819 had reached 5,000.

To these were added the nonconformist Lancasterian schools, with a boys' school opening in 1812. Financed by voluntary contributions and the school pence paid by parents, the school was managed by a committee of subscribers that at various times included Albert Hill and members of the Forster family. It was named after the educational system devised by Andrew Bell and Joseph Lancaster which allowed large numbers of children to be taught by one teacher. Learning was broken into small chunks taught to the older pupils or monitors, and the pupils themselves could then pass this on to the younger ones. Using this system, the Lancasterian boys' school could take on a roll of 141 boys in 1820 and 172 by 1840. It started in temporary accommodation and in 1822 moved to a new building on the south side of Church Road.

Lancasterian girls' school never had such large numbers of pupils, with just 79 in 1821 and an average attendance between 90 and 100. It opened in 1815 on the corner of the High Road and Reform Row, and like the boys' school was managed by a committee, although in this case the 14 ladies came under the overall management of the boys' school. It was financed the same way, with the addition of a small income from the sale of the girls' needlework, although it often needed subsidising from the boys' school. William Robinson in his *History* noted with satisfaction that the girls were taught the 'common and useful branches of learning and needlework' and their instruction aimed 'to promote the future usefulness and benefit of those who are educated in this school'. When

they left at 14 they went into service or other 'suitable employment'.

A number of other voluntary schools were established in Tottenham during the 19th century, mostly aligned to one particular church or another and reflecting the growth of the village. All Hallows boys school was opened in 1841 in Marsh Lane (later Park Lane), becoming St Paul's National School in

75 *An 1872 leaflet published as part of the campaign against establishing a School Board, which would bring in nondenominational schools and lead to a probable increase in the rates.*

Parishioners of Tottenham !

BEWARE ! GUARD AGAINST DECEPTION !!!

THE BLUE SCHOOL is the Property of Subscribers. It is not Denominational; all Subscribers to its funds have a voice in its Management.

Churchmen of Tottenham !

You freely and liberally agreed to parish property being given for the Congregational Church on the Green; and you would do so again.

Dissenters of Tottenham !

Will you oppose the Enlargement of a *Parish School,* open to *all,* because it has hitherto been chiefly supported by Churchmen ? Surely not.

Ratepayers of Tottenham !

The object of Enlarging the Blue School is to *avoid* a School Board and the consequent *enormous increase of rating!* Do you want to be further taxed? No! Attend the Poll, then, on WEDNESDAY NEXT at the Lecture Hall (from 8 to 10 and 4 till 9), and Vote

FOR THE RESOLUTION
Proposed by the Rev. H. McSorley.

A Fragment.

S.   What I dread most is this,
Lest Churchmen here should *ostracise* our bairns,
And taint their minds with Catechisms.

W.   Never,
While through my veins the blood of Scotland flows !
Rather I'd see them lie at Manning's feet
Bound hand and foot.

F.   Well spoken. We are men of principle !!!

T. B.   Principle ! Gentlemen, I beg to move an Amendment.

76 *Fowler Newsam, who campaigned against the setting up of a Board of Education. In spite of his support for building denominational elementary schools, these were not enough to meet growing needs.*

1875. In 1870 St Paul's National School for girls and infants was opened in Park Lane on land leased from the parish charity estate. The church of Holy Trinity at High Cross opened an infants' school in 1848, whilst the Hermitage school in Hanger Lane (now St Ann's Road) for girls, boys and infants opened in 1848. This school, separating into three buildings in 1863 (boys) and 1871 (girls), was largely financed by Fowler Newsam (d.1875), who lived in the High Road on Stamford Hill. He also paid for most of the church of St Ann's, along with the vicarage and some model cottages. The Hermitage schools were later renamed St Ann's, after the church.

In 1827 a small Catholic school was opened for boys, girls and infants, close to the new church of St Francis de Sales in Chapel Place. The church had been erected by Baroness de Montesquiere to replace a temporary chapel

run by a French emigrant clergyman, the Rev. Le Tellier, and is a reflection of the number of French immigrants to the village since the time of the French Revolution. The church's congregation, according to William Robinson, increased in summer due to an 'influx of strangers into Tottenham, principally Irish', who were clearly here for harvest work. St Francis school was enlarged and moved to Brereton Road in 1882, and by 1886 there were separate boys', girls' and infants' schools.

The one-room Edmonton and Tottenham Ragged School, established by Dr Michael Laseron (who also founded the Prince of Wales Hospital), was opened in 1858 in Snells Park, Edmonton. With additional income from a bequest from Thomas Knight, a larger building was opened by Lord Shaftesbury in Union Row, Tottenham, close to the Edmonton border, and became known as the Ragged and Industrial Home. It later moved to Pembroke House in the High Road and closed down around 1890.

AN INSUFFICIENCY OF PLACES

In spite of these new schools, provision hardly kept up with the increase in population, and certainly could not meet the needs of all in the community. There was national recognition that a basic education should be made available to all to support literacy, numeracy and, it was hoped, discipline and good morals. In 1872 William Forster introduced his Education Act, and parishes or boroughs were required to ensure there were enough school places for

77   *Page Green schools, Broad Lane, c.1907. The building has now been demolished and the site used for housing.*

children, and, if not, to establish an elected School Board with the power to raise additional rates. By 1880 compulsory school attendance to the age of 10 put additional pressure on ensuring provision.

With the doubling of the population between 1870 and 1880, Tottenham was clearly deficient in school places, but there was considerable resistance to a School Board. The local newspaper campaigned vociferously against a Board, worried about the likely increase in rates, whilst individuals such as Fowler Newsam and the vicar of St Paul's led the campaign to prevent the establishment of non-sectarian schools. More energy was put into fund raising, and some improvements were made, but with an estimated deficiency of over 2,000 places in 1879, the Education Department ordered a local Board to be set up.

Once elected, the Board set to work with considerable vigour. A number of temporary schools were established, using rooms and halls hired from nonconformist churches, but there was also a rapid spate of new school building over the last two decades of the century. These schools were immense compared to anything previously built. The buildings usually had separate boys', girls' and infant schools, each with their own headteacher, and accommodated over 1,500 pupils altogether. They were mostly two-storey buildings, usually with a main building housing the girls on the ground floor and the boys on the first floor, and a separate single-storey infant school. Occasionally the three-tiered school, with infants, girls and boys layered one on top of the other, such as Seven Sisters or Noel Park, was erected.

The first board school to be built was Coleraine Park, opened in 1881 for 1,152 pupils, although in the early days it often exceeded that number. Over the next two decades eight new schools were built, including Page Green and Stamford Hill in 1882, West Green (1886), Seven Sisters (1889), Downhills (1893), Bruce Grove (1894), Earlsmead (1897) and Woodlands Park in 1900. In addition the Lancasterian schools moved to the School Board in 1887, and a new school was built in Kings Road.

The Tottenham School Board was also responsible for Wood Green, and during this period built White Hart Lane (1884), Bounds Green (1888), Noel Park (1889) and Alexandra (1895) schools. Wood Green and Tottenham became separate Part II Education Authorities in 1903 following the 1902 Education Act.

During its brief lifetime the Board established 15 new schools, most of them taking in over 1,500 pupils. Many of these schools experienced difficult beginnings, with overcrowding and fluctuating rolls caused by the mobile population. A number of these schools continue today, variously altered, extended and sometimes rebuilt, but they are now mixed primaries catering for many fewer pupils. In spite of this continuity, they are evidence, in their change of use and size over the years, of changing developments in state education practice.

78   *Rt Hon W.E. Forster, MP, educated in Tottenham and a member of the local Forster family. He was instrumental in getting the 1870 Education Act passed, and with it elementary education for all children.*

EIGHT

Carriers and Commuters

Traffic continued to grow along the High Road, but on the eastern edge of the village attempts were being made to bypass the crowded and poorly maintained road by using the River Lea. London merchants had long seen the lengthy river as another route for transporting their goods, but there were many challenges to making the Lea an efficient waterway. The meanders, overgrown banks, silting and blockages, as well as shallow rapids interspersed with deep pools, all hindered travel. A series of Navigation Acts, starting in Elizabeth's reign, were initiated to clear the waterway. Artificial cuts were devised to avoid the worst shallows and meanders, and local residents instructed to scour the river of obstructions and clear the banks.

People did not always take kindly to these instructions, particularly when they affected their own interests. Fishermen had their traps and sandbanks, osiers their reed beds and farmers wished to preserve the periodic flooding that enriched their water meadows. The millers, with their weirs and millstreams, controlled the water's flow and depth. Boatmen needed the co-operation of mill-owners for their journey, but did not always get it. In 1666, for example, Thomas Worrill of Tottenham Mills drained the river so low that 14 barges were

grounded, whilst Worrill demanded excess fees to free them. The maltmen from Enfield bitterly opposed the loss of their transport monopoly through the use of boats by London brewers. Improvements made to the waterway were sabotaged and sometimes violence broke out between the conflicting interests.

A few cuts were made over the years, bypassing the worst of the shallows where the Lea crossed Tottenham marshes, splitting the area into a number of islands, such as Mill Mead in the south and the Great Holme in the north. The biggest improvement, however, followed the 1767 Navigation Act, when canal engineer John Smeaton constructed a series of 14 cuts from Hertford to the Thames to create the River Lea Navigation. In spite of objections from the local Vestry, a canal was made through Tottenham, running from Enfield Mills to Tottenham Mills and cutting off Mitchley Marsh and splitting the Wild Marsh in two. The canal was later extended west of the mill to join the main river at Ferry Lane, where Tottenham Lock was constructed.

The Navigation was now 'an efficient artery of commerce', and it continued to transport heavy goods until the second half of the 20th century, when it made the slow transition from commercial to leisure use.

79   *Tottenham Mills in 1840. Planted firmly on the River Lea, and using channels to control the flow of water, mills such as these were a hindrance to efficient water transport.*

'... THIS ROAD IS EXCEEDINGLY THRONGED'

For people, though, as well as many goods, the High Road remained the preferred route, as Daniel Defoe noted in 1726. But it was seldom easy to travel along, especially when it rained and the gravel surface sank into the clay under the pressure of the traffic. Maintenance work was carried out by parishioners, who were required to do four full days work a year on the highways or employ labourers to do it, and the quality of the work was debatable. A further hazard for road travellers in the 18th century was the danger imposed by highwaymen when it was dark. In 1774 petitioners complained to Parliament that the road was 'very dangerous and inconvenient in the winter season, being often in the night time infested with robbers, which might, in a great measure, be prevented if the road was lighted and a proper guard put thereon'.

There were a number of problems to be dealt with before the main highways could become safe and efficient. Parishes resented having to maintain a road that was used as much, if not more, by

passing traffic than local residents, and the use of local untrained and unqualified men was not always efficient. The introduction of turnpike trusts placed the costs of road maintenance on the road users through turnpike tolls, and brought main highways under more professional management, with paid officers. The Stamford Hill and Green Lanes Turnpike Trust was set up following petitions in 1713 and road maintenance gradually improved along the main highways. By the 19th century the quality of the roads was further improved by using the methods of engineers such as Thomas Telford and James Macadam, introducing solid foundations, good drainage and stronger road surfaces.

From 1774 the Turnpike Trust introduced watching and lighting on the highway during the winter months, making a difference to the safety and usability of the roads. The introduction of effective lighting was gradual, the oil used in 1774 being replaced by gas from 1815. By 1863 there were 60 gas lamps placed along the High Road, although at first these were only lit for nine months of the year. Watchmen were hired to patrol the roads and to 'prevent all mischiefs by fire, and all burglaries, murders and other outrages…'. They also had powers to apprehend any 'nightwalkers, rogues or vagabonds' seen loitering or misbehaving or suspected of 'evil design'. Eventually the Turnpike Trust passed into the hands of the Commissioners of the Metropolitan Turnpike Roads in 1826, and in 1888 the new county councils took over responsibility. From 1840 law enforcement was taken over by the Metropolitan Police, with a remit wider than the main highways.

But these improvements scarcely kept pace with the dramatic increase in traffic, as covered wagons, horses, carts, private carriages and coaches pounded the High Road. By the 1830s stage coaches travelled daily from the City to Cambridge, Hertford, Lincoln and York, with Tottenham travellers waiting at the *Ship Inn* in the High Road for their connection. From 1823 local commuter services were introduced and by 1840 Tottenham had a half-hourly service to and from London, the last coach leaving London at 10.20 p.m. It was now possible for professional residents of Tottenham to work in London, as did Edwin Hill of Bruce Castle, who commuted daily on the hour-long service to his office in the City.

In 1829 George Shillibeer introduced his horse-drawn omnibus, making way for the big companies such as the London General Omnibus Company to provide commuter services. But

there were also small local businesses, among these being Mr Willan of Tottenham Hale who ran a daily three-horse private omnibus from Shoreditch to the Angel, Edmonton, taking a regular set of local businessmen. In between journeys Mr Willan attended customers in his hairdressing salon. With the opening of the new Seven Sisters road in 1833 another local tradesman, Mr Warren, started a service to west London, running three times a day from the Hale to Regents Park.

In 1870 the Metropolitan Tramway Company laid a track through Tottenham, eliminating most locally run businesses. Trams now dominated road transport, providing efficient services to the less well paid and enabling more residents to travel for shopping, entertainment and work. They continued as the backbone of public road transport until the 1930s, moving briefly in the 1880s to unpopular steam power, and becoming electrified in 1904.

CATTLE AND COMMUTERS

The first railway to run through the village was as early as 1840, when the Northern and Eastern Railway opened the line from Broxbourne to Shoreditch, crossing the eastern edge along the marshes. The company took 53 acres of Lammas land on payment of £650, and agreed to make a rail bridge over the lane running from the

80 *Horse bus, c.1890, possibly photographed at the bottom of Stamford Hill where an extra horse was needed for the gradient.*

81 *Late 19th-century horse tram at the corner of Seven Sisters Road. Horse trams were soon to be superseded by steam power for a short while, and then by electricity in 1904.*

marshes to Down Lane, and a level crossing for animals and carts coming from the marshes. Stations were opened at Northumberland Park and Tottenham Hale, but for the most part they were too remote for local passengers. The line, eventually extended to Cambridge, was used mainly for transporting animals from the countryside into London, and 40 cattle pens, holding 30 animals each, were erected at Tottenham Hale station. But, in 1847 Queen Victoria and Prince Albert came to Tottenham Hale to board their royal train to Cambridge, and the visit was accompanied by a great local fanfare, including bands, cavalry and a specially built pavilion by the station.

In 1872 the Enfield to Liverpool Street line was opened, with stations at White Hart Lane, Bruce Grove and Seven Sisters. Running through the centre of Tottenham, closely following the High Road and offering workmen's fares of 1s. weekly, the line had a dramatic impact on the population, in relation to both its growth and class. The fast and cheap service from the suburbs to the city made it possible for clerks, workmen and tradesmen to move out of inner London's congested streets into the semi-rural

82 *Car No. 18, a steam tram* c.*1880 from Finsbury Park to Ponders End, with an advertisement for G.L. Wilson, a successful local builders' merchant, on the side. These trams were unpopular because of the dirt they produced.*

83 *Tottenham Hale station in 1855, painted by James F. Vickery in 1943. The Northern and Eastern Railway line was important for transporting livestock to the London market.*

northern districts. Writing of Tottenham at this time, a contemporary report noted that 'the Clerk and warehouseman in the city makes his home here ... rents here are exceptionally moderate, so that most deserving of all classes, the struggling clerk with a large family, may become possessed of a charming cottage or villa ... at less rent than he would pay for two or three rooms in Clerkenwell.'

HOUSING THE NEW RESIDENTS

The effect of the railway on Tottenham's population was dramatic. From 9,120 in 1851 it grew to a staggering 71,343 in 1891 – and this was without Wood Green, now a separate administrative authority. The rate of migration, always significant in Tottenham's history, gathered pace. People moved in from villages across the country, confident they could find work in overcrowded London and live within commuting distance, whilst families from the city's congested streets moved to the more open spaces of the suburbs. Keeping pace with the population growth led to a housing boom, as speculative builders, large and small, erected houses on Tottenham's former farmland and the

grounds of the great estates. The large houses gave up their land, Row's House, Markfield, West Green House, Woodlands, Downhills and Mount Pleasant being sold off between 1879 and 1890. Wealthy landowners moved out, the workmen, labourers, clerks and teachers moved in, and Tottenham shifted to a predominantly lower middle- and working-class area.

South Tottenham was the first to receive the newcomers, with streets and houses growing up in the fields around St Ann's and West Green roads, Philip Lane and across the High Road to Broad Lane, High Cross Road and Tottenham Hale. In the standardised stock-brick terraces, houses stood 40 to an acre 'with back gardens distinctly minimal and front gardens merely nominal'. Some of the housing was poor, jerry-built, and criticised by commentators as having no adequate foundations, walls half a brick thick and no proper surface drainage. But even the meanest of these homes probably bore comparison to the older timber-framed working-class housing that remained. The courts and alleys of Scotland Green, a maze of tiny cottages, some built back-to-back and close to the open stream of the Carbuncle ditch, were home to numerous poor families, and the

84   *Downhills House in 1884, one of the many grand houses demolished to make way for the new terraced streets. Fortunately the grounds were saved to become Downhills Park.*

densely packed houses along Whitehall Road, Love Lane and Wagon Lane achieved notoriety for their conditions and the unsociable nature of their residents.

Not far from Scotland Green was the Coleraine Park estate, built between 1870 and 1880 on farmland and the former Mockings Manor. It stretched from the Carbuncle stream in the south to Park Lane in the north. The land had been bought by speculators and the plots were developed as a mixture of larger villas and smaller terraced houses. The terraces were built south of Lansdowne Road by the Northern and Eastern Suburban Industrial Development Company with the intention of offering tenants and purchasers 'good property at a moderate

85   *Love Lane in north Tottenham in 1934, shortly before slum clearance. This narrow street, with doorways straight onto the pavement, was a notorious area of overcrowding and poverty and was probably built for the workers in the Church Road lace factory.*

cost'. The company avoided the problem of bankruptcy faced by single builders if their houses did not sell, being in a position to retain property for rent. These were solid houses with good sized gardens, but being just west of the marshes, the estate was sometimes cold and damp, often abandoned by families in the winter. The headmistress of the local school complained about frequent absences and the 'migratory nature' of her pupils.

North of the terraced houses were the grander streets of Lansdowne and St Pauls roads, and their more substantial houses, meeting up with Marsh Lane (now more elegantly named Park Lane). At its eastern end Park Lane joined with Northumberland Park, where semi-detached villas had been erected in the 1860s. Villas were also built along West Green Road and Philip Lane, and from the 1880s the Mount Pleasant estate was developed. These larger and better built homes, with three or four bedrooms, a bathroom and good sized gardens, attracted clerks earning perhaps £100 to £130 a year, who considered themselves socially superior to the

86 *This photograph by Hunnings, the photographers of Broomfield Villa, Philip Lane, c.1870, shows an example of the larger villas erected in Tottenham in the latter part of the 19th century which were alongside terraces of working-class housing.*

tradesmen, artisans and factory workers filling the terraced streets in other parts of Tottenham. Builders' advertisements pointed out that these houses had 'the right address'.

87 *Holy Trinity church, showing the small Infant and Sunday school building, with the well in front. Holy Trinity, established in 1830, was Tottenham's second parish church.*

88 *St Ignatius church, south Tottenham, built in 1903,*
was Tottenham's second Catholic church, after St Francis
de Sales at the northern end of the High Road.

89 *St Ann's church and school, c.1870. The building of the*
church and schools was largely financed by Fowler Newsam.

NEW PLACES TO PRAY

Church building followed the housing growth, with Tottenham's second parish church of Holy Trinity, on the Green by Philip Lane, established in 1830. In nearby Hanger Lane (now St Ann's Road), the richly designed church of St Ann's, founded in 1860, was largely financed by the businessman Fowler Newsam, and catered for wealthier families in the district. In north Tottenham, St Paul's church in Park Lane was consecrated in 1859, meeting the needs of the largely middle-class villas erected in Northumberland Park and Park Lane. On the other hand, St Mary's church on Lansdowne Road, opened in 1887, catered largely for the working-class communities living on Coleraine estate and around Scotland Green and Factory Lane. It was partly funded from the Marlborough College mission, and the Church also ran three mission halls in the area.

A Jesuit college was established at Stamford Hill in 1894, with the chapel of St Ignatius attached. In 1903 the imposing church of St Ignatius was built to replace the chapel, and complemented St Francis de Sales, further north along the High Road. Churches, chapels and mission halls of nonconformist groups were established across the town. Apart from the Quakers, there were large congregations of Methodists, Baptists, Congregationalists, the Brethren and the Salvation Army. By 1903, half of religious attendance on a Sunday represented nonconformist groups. Towards the end of the 19th century another small religious group had started worshipping in people's homes, but in 1904 the Tottenham Hebrew Congregation opened a small synagogue in the High Road on the corner of Somerset Road.

NINE

Meeting the Challenges

Tottenham's population rose steadily throughout the 19th century, from 3,622 in 1801 to 71,343 in 1891, and as the parish moved from a sprawling village to a town, the pressures on the local community grew too much for the Vestry to manage alone. Gradually it devolved its power to other authorities, such as the Metropolitan Police in 1840. The main devolution, however, came in 1850 when Tottenham was one of the first areas in Middlesex to take powers under the 1848 Public Health Act and establish a permanent local Board of Health. The Board became responsible for the general health and safety of the parish, including lighting, fire-fighting, water and sewerage.

Starting with a body of nine members in 1850, numbers rose to 12 in 1871 and 15 in 1888, as a rise in population west of the High Road resulted in the addition of West Green and St Ann's wards. Meanwhile, Wood Green residents had argued for separation from Tottenham, correctly realising that their needs were not so critical, and they achieved a Board of their own in 1888. Wood Green, with a population of 23,000, was now formally divided from Tottenham, with its population of 65,000. In 1894 the Board became an Urban District Council under the Local Government Act, with five wards electing five members every three years. This changed to annual elections in 1900, with one member retiring from each ward yearly. By 1901 Harringay ward had been created in the south west, and by 1905 the Council had 30 members.

CLEAN WATER AND PROPER SANITATION

Tottenham Board of Health faced exceptional challenges in supporting a growing urban community. In 1840 most of the public water supplies came from four local wells, including the well by Holy Trinity church which is still standing today and is an early example of the William Morris Arts and Crafts movement. The wells were dug to a deeper level than formerly, penetrating through the clay to produce an apparently inexhaustible supply of pure spring water. By 1853 the board claimed it had provided a full water supply in all built-up areas, but three years later it had to extend its works at the Hale. This inadvertently drew water from the local marshland which was periodically flooded by filthy streams emptying into the Lea, a blunder not apparently realised until 1873.

The underground water supply faltered from 1864, and was so intermittent from 1867 that the wealthy made their own arrangements with the water companies for piped water, and others resorted to carriers, cisterns and private wells. In 1872 the Board took matters in hand to ensure an adequate provision. Dismissing advice to go to the water companies, it installed a pump at the works in 1876, providing Tottenham with purer water than its neighbours. By 1883 it was possible to close the well and pump at Tottenham Green. Further work included a tower next to the reservoir in Hill Pond field at Downhills in 1883, and in 1892 Longwater pumping station on the Wild Marsh was opened.

Access to water from the Lea was, however, limited as the New River Company and East London Waterworks Company had virtual monopoly over its water. The local board became partly dependent on these two companies from 1880. From 1897 to 1904, the Banbury and Lockwood reservoirs were built over the marshes on the eastern side of the navigation, taking Mitchley Marsh and a large part of Wild Marsh East. Finally, in 1904, the Metropolitan Water Board took over from the different authorities and companies and managed the entire area.

There were just as many challenges in ensuring adequate sewerage in the district.

Two main problems continually defeated the best efforts, relentless house building and the torrent of sewage coming down from Hornsey and Wood Green. Many houses did not have adequate sewage disposal, and 800 houses were still discharging their waste into the Moselle in 1848. The effluent from the Moselle and other streams rising in the west ended up in the river Lea, frequently flooding over onto the low-lying lands on the east of the parish and giving rise to a stinking, unhealthy morass.

The Board started well enough, building tanks and filter beds at works near Markfield Road and contracting with a manure manufacturer to treat the sewage. This worked efficiently until the contractor died suddenly in 1858 and sewage started to dissipate in land around Page Green and discharge into the Lea. There were accusations that Tottenham's sewage polluted the East London Company's water supply and contributed to the deaths of thousands in the East End. Tottenham's health was no better, and in 1871 was showing a death rate of 21.4 per thousand, worse than any area outside east London. Parochialism stood in the way of sorting the problem of sewage from Hornsey and Wood Green, and there was deadlock over plans to pipe waste to costly irrigation works at Walthamstow.

90 *The fountain opposite the Bell and Hare in 1821. This was erected by the parish in the early part of the 19th century as one of four wells, but they soon became inadequate in the face of the growing population.*

91   *The water tower next to the reservoir in Hill Pond field, Downhills Road, seen here in 1923, was built by the local Board of Health in 1883.*

It was 1871 before improvements started to make a difference. A pipe was built along Lordship Lane from Wood Green, and after Hornsey constructed its own sewer the Moselle was properly cleansed. A contract was agreed with the Chemical Manure Company for treatment of sewage at Markfield Road, which was now jointly run by Tottenham and Wood Green. In 1880 there were still concerns over the increasing amounts of sewage finding its way into the River Lea and proposals were made to increase the capacity of the tanks and the rate of treatment with a new pumping engine. A new

beam engine was opened in 1888, transferring some four million gallons of sewage over a 24 hour period to the London Northern Outfall works at Becton. After 1891 responsibility for sewerage passed from Tottenham to Northern High Level sewer in Hackney, when this became part of the LCC's main drainage system. By 1893 the Lea Conservancy could report that 'fish are now numerous in the river below the Tottenham Sewage Works'.

TOWARDS A SAFER COMMUNITY

Fires had always been a hazard, and in spite of the improvements with engines and pumps were still difficult to extinguish. Albert Hill of Bruce Castle recalls in 1839 when the rubber factory in the High Road caught fire, creating a glorious blaze as the naphtha used for dissolving rubber erupted like volcanoes. The new parish fire engine was of little help as its hose was too short to reach the nearby brook. One of the resourceful Hill brothers organised a double line of spectators to fill the engine by the use of buckets, exhausting work that took several hours but did not save the factory. Some fifteen years later a fire at Church Farm (now the Priory, Church Lane) attracted many fire engines from neighbouring parishes, including the head of the London Fire Brigade, and the blaze was successfully tackled.

An engineer in charge of fire-fighting was elected on an annual basis, and in 1838 the Vestry ordered a new parish engine, probably not much more than a horse-drawn cart with a pump and hose for applying water. In 1854 there was still only one engine, kept at the Watch House on Scotland Green. Responsibility for maintaining the engine and using it when required lay with the superintendent, at the time parish beadle John Fowler. It was claimed he did not look after the engine, that it was seldom cleaned and frequently out of order. Its performance at one fire in 1866 was lamentable,

92   *An 1886 compound condensing beam engine installed in the Markfield sewage works. This engine could process four million gallons every 24 hours.*

undertakings to become the Tottenham District Light, Heat and Power Co. in 1914. Its impressive showrooms on the corner of the High Road and Lordship Lane were opened in 1901 selling gas appliances to local communities. Local houses were now more safely lit by gas, and gas for heating and cooking was gradually being introduced.

Streets had also been made safer by the introduction of the Metropolitan Police in Tottenham in 1840. By 1908 the Watch House had been replaced by two stations in Tottenham, the main one at 398 High Road on the corner of Chesnut Road, and another in St Ann's Road. The High Road station was rebuilt in 1913 and still stands today, but the old station was the scene of a particularly violent robbery that went horribly wrong, and has been known ever since as the 'Tottenham Outrage'.

Two armed men tried to rob the payroll from Schurmann's factory in Chesnut Road, nearly opposite the station. They escaped with the money by running to the marshes, across into Walthamstow and finally ending up in Hale End, Chingford. They were chased by a crowd of up to 100 policemen and a number of civilians, in cars, on foot and on horse. At various stages the robbers hijacked a tram, a milk cart and a greengrocer's cart, all the time firing shots at the chasing crowd. In the process they killed a ten-year-old boy, Ralph Joscelyn, in Chesnut Road, and a policeman, William Tyler, in Down Lane (now Park View Road), by the refuse works. At the end of the chase the robbers turned their guns on themselves, one dying in a cottage in

arriving hours after the fire broke out, the hose not connected, and Fowler going straight off to the local public house to 'treat the men'.

But it was the 1870s before more effective systems were put in place, with a new engine house at Coombes Croft and a volunteer fire brigade set up by public subscription in 1870, which became a professional paid force in 1892. In 1892 a manual engine with fire escape and curricle was installed, and in 1903 the first petrol motor traction in the country was introduced at the new Conway Road fire station. In 1905 the central fire station was opened next to the town hall on Tottenham Green, and was soon to house the magnificent fire engine designed for the Council by Mr Zwicky in 1906.

Street lighting gradually became more reliable and widespread, particularly after 1847 when gas was supplied by the new Tottenham and Edmonton Gas and Light Company. The company eventually absorbed neighbouring

Hale End, and the other, eventually, in the Prince of Wales Hospital. The men were later identified as Latvians connected with Russian anarchist and revolutionary groups, but whether it was politics or money that motivated them is not known.

HEALTH CARE

There were a number of local doctors and midwives offering their services during the 19th century, such as the Quaker May family, who served Tottenham for two generations. The cost of a doctor's visit could be prohibitive for poorer people, but the establishment of the Tottenham and Edmonton Dispensary in 1864 provided help for many. It was opened to members (working people and servants, and their wives and children) for a payment of

93 *Model of Tottenham's early fire engine and pump, c.1840, which usually proved woefully inadequate in the event of a big fire.*

94 *The Merryweather oil-fuelled fire engine at Harringay fire station in 1905, one of the earliest examples of a motor traction engine.*

95   *The old Tottenham Police Station on the corner of Chesnut Road and the High Road, before being rebuilt in 1913. This station was the scene of a violent wage-snatch in January 1909 that culminated in a dramatic chase across the marshes to Chingford, and the deaths of a boy, a policeman and the two robbers.*

1d. a week, 3d. for families and 5s. a year for servants. This entitled members to see one of the local doctors who attended the Dispensary on rotation every morning except Sundays. If members needed medicine they had to take along their own bottles. Doctors also attended confinements, and members' children were entitled to free vaccinations. The services of the Dispensary had been free at first, supported by church collections, but it remained possible for poor non-members to see a Dispensary doctor, providing they had a doctor's letter. By 1907 there were 941 members, nearly half representing families, and in 1910 the premises were rebuilt. The Dispensary remained in use until 1938, and the 1910 building still stands in front of the Spurs stadium.

Dr Laseron (d.1894) established the Evangelical Protestant Deaconesses' Institute for training nurses, originally those from his orphanage, but soon including girls from 'good families'. In 1869 the Institute moved into Avenue House on the south-east side of Tottenham Green and opened as a hospital. The building was replaced in 1881 and further extensions added in 1887. By this time it was treating 721 inpatients (51 private) and 7,836 outpatients annually.

From 1899 the voluntary deaconesses were replaced by paid and certificated nurses, and the hospital became a district hospital. In 1901 it had 73 beds serving a north London population of 300,000. It was then called the Tottenham Hospital, but in 1907, after enlargement, it was renamed the Prince of Wales general hospital in recognition of the fact that it served a wider area than Tottenham. A convalescence home in Nazeing, Essex was given to the hospital in 1914, and buildings around the hospital were acquired in 1917. Further extensions were made over the years, until in 1985 it was closed during another bout of hospital reorganisation. The handsome buildings, including the houses flanking the hospital, have been retained and it now serves the locality as housing.

The hospital was largely supported by fundraising events and donations from individuals and organisations such as the Prince of Wales Hospital Fund for London. This later became the King Edward Fund, then simply the King's Fund. Fund raising also came from local activities such as concerts, dinners and cricket matches. The annual Pound Day involved local people donating either a pound in money or a pound in weight of a wide variety of goods, including tea, sugar, flour, biscuits and cleaning products.

The most popular fundraising event, however, was the Tottenham Carnival, a street parade of decorated horse-drawn carts and carriages, accompanied by walkers, many of them children in fancy dress, which made its way down the High Road, now decorated with bunting. It was started by local cricket clubs around 1898, and then run by ward committees. The Carnival was still raising money for the hospital up until the Second World War, and continues today as an annual community festival.

During earlier plagues and epidemics, Tottenham had avoided a 'pox house', or fever hospital, apart from occasional temporary buildings during outbreaks. Cholera had largely been tackled by the late 19th century thanks to better sanitation and smallpox was not the scourge it used to be thanks to vaccination, but there was still a number of contagious diseases around. Containment was often the answer, with sufferers isolated in fever hospitals. In 1892, during an

96   *The 'Tottenham Tragedy', showing the spot where PC Tyler was shot dead. Tyler was one of two people killed by the robbers, the other being a ten-year-old boy, Ralph Joscelyne. The incident is now generally know as the 'Outrage'.*

epidemic of scarlet fever, the Metropolitan Asylums Board opened temporary buildings for the North-East Fever Hospital on the south side of St Ann's Road, despite considerable local opposition. The buildings were made into permanent blocks by 1900, covering 19 acres of land once in the possession of Clerkenwell Abbey and later the Knights of St John. In 1948 the hospital became St Ann's General Hospital, and the scattered buildings in their extensive grounds are still in use today, no longer as a general hospital but responding to particular needs such as mental health, paediatrics and eyesight.

Another hospital was built in the High Road near the town hall. The Jewish Home and Hospital for Incurables offered care and religious facilities to poor Jews and was funded by charity donations. There was a considerable community of Jews in Tottenham, who undoubtedly helped with the funding and building of this hospital, but it was established in 1889 to provide long-term care for Jews across London. The new

97   *Dr Edward Curtis May, c.1870, who started practising in Tottenham in 1822 when he was one of only two doctors in the parish. He was succeeded by his son Dr E. Hooper May.*

buildings were opened in 1903 in the more rural surroundings of Tottenham High Road, where there were also good transport links for visiting relatives. The three-storey red-brick building included a concert hall and later a synagogue. Designed for 80 patients, it was extended in 1914 with an additional 34 beds. A

98   *Tottenham Dispensary, c.1902, decorated for the Tottenham Carnival. The Dispensary building, where members could see a doctor for a minimal subscription fee, still stands, empty, in front of the Spurs ground.*

nurses' home was built in 1938 and a new block in 1964, by which time it was catering for 114 patients. The hospital closed in 1995 and, like the Prince of Wales, the substantial building has been converted into housing, set back from the High Road and in its own grounds.

CIVIC AMENITIES AND CIVIC PRIDE

Following 1894, when Tottenham became an Urban District Council, there was a shift in the development of the town. The large old houses on the west side of Tottenham Green, Eaton House, Wilton House, Hatfield House and The Ferns, were bought by the Council for civic purposes. In 1905 the town hall was opened on the site, a red-brick building with stone dressing in a Baroque style. Flanking the hall were the central fire station and the public baths, of similar red brick but plainer. In 1913 they were joined by the county grammar school, and this handsome row of buildings,

99 *Dr Michael Laseron, founder of the Prince of Wales Hospital, formerly the Evangelical Protestant Deaconness Institute for training nurses.*

100 *The Prince of Wales soon became an important local hospital, and then a district hospital. This picture shows the Victoria Mary children's ward in 1924.*

101   *Three men dressed up for Tottenham Carnival in 1909 (Weary Willy, Tired Tim and the Laziest Man in Tottenham), with their Tottenham Hospital collecting boxes.*

still retaining the open green in front, made an imposing municipal centre.

The buildings were evidence of new civic pride, but also practicality. The public baths included two swimming pools and the 'slipper' baths. For many local people, with just an outdoor toilet, bathing was only possible using zinc baths in the kitchen, laboriously filled with kettles of hot water. There was no privacy and the water was often used several times. The slipper baths provided private cubicles with good-sized baths filled with hot water. There were 18 baths for men and 12 for women, divided in the fashion

102   *A bird's eye view of the North Eastern Hospital (later St Ann's) shortly after the permanent buildings were erected.*

of the day into first and second class. The two swimming pools were also first and second class, one being smaller than the other, and special sessions for ladies were offered in the afternoons and Wednesday and Saturday mornings. During the winter the baths were boarded over for concerts and dances.

These buildings still stand, but their use has changed considerably. The county school is used by the local college and the baths, largely rebuilt behind the frontage, are now the Bernie Grant Arts Centre, named after the popular MP for Tottenham from 1987 to 2000. The fire station is used by voluntary organisations, and the old town hall is currently undergoing refurbishment to be used for workshops and voluntary groups.

Further down the High Road, opposite the High Cross, the central lending library was opened in 1896. Tottenham adopted the Public Libraries Act in 1891, opening temporary reading rooms at Eaton House and, in 1900, more reading rooms at the Chestnuts in St Ann's Road. The St Ann's rooms were soon converted to a lending library and moved to the new

103   *The Jewish Home and Hospital in south Tottenham, 1907.*

education offices in Philip Lane in 1917, moving to its final home in Vincent Road in 1931 when it became West Green Library. Coombes Croft library was opened in 1925 in the old parish workhouse, and by the 1930s two more branch libraries were added, St Ann's in Cissbury Road (1931) and Devonshire Hill in Compton Crescent (1935). For many local residents, the libraries offered access to knowledge and education as well as leisure.

104   *The main entrance lobby of the central library in 1931.*

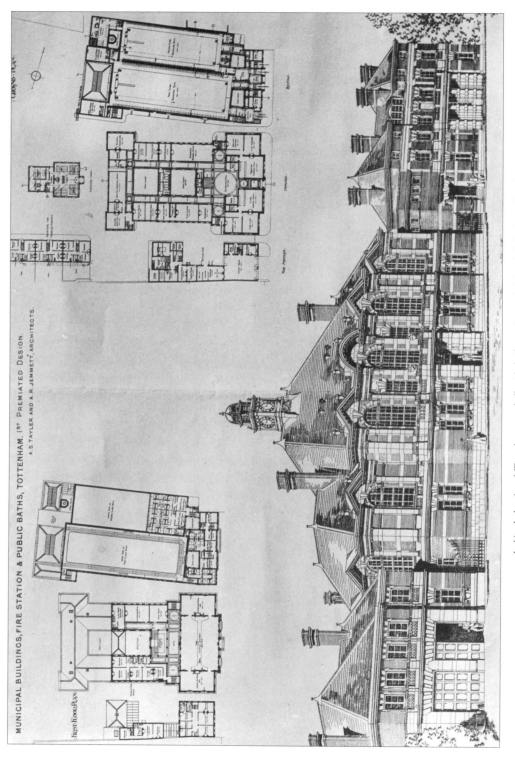

105   *Architect's drawing of Tottenham town hall, with the fire station on the left and the baths on the right.*

Ten

A Working Town

lthough many residents commuted to London to work, there was a considerable amount of local employment in industry, commerce and agriculture. Industry in Tottenham had used the River Lea since the Middle Ages. Apart from the flour mill, there were mills for fulling cloth in the 15th century, leather and paper in the 17th century, then corn and oil mills through to their demise in a fire in 1860.

FROM POTTERIES TO ENGINEERING

The brickearth in the west of the parish was exploited sporadically from the 15th century, but it was in the 19th that the local clay was used more extensively. In 1856 Williamson's Potteries were in Green Lanes, later the site of Harringay Stadium and, more recently, Sainsbury's superstore. These potteries were closed in 1905, at which time the site was stagnant ponds and muddy fields, often flooded by a local stream. The nearby workers' cottages were condemned by the local Medical Officer of Health as unfit for habitation. One son of a pottery worker in the cottages was E.G. Cole. His father had established Tottenham Potteries along White Hart Lane some time in the 1870s, and E.G. Cole went on to turn the potteries

into a thriving business, making pots for the nursery and market garden trade.

Neighbouring Cole's in White Hart Lane were the equally successful South family potteries. Samuel South took over the firm in 1896 and, like Cole's, produced mainly flower pots, using the traditional hand forming technique. Both potteries closed in the 1950s, and that stretch of White Hart Lane now includes the site of St George's industrial estate.

The first factory arrived in Tottenham in 1810 when William Herbert of Nottingham opened his lace factory in Love Lane close to Church Road. He extended it in 1833, when he bought the remainder of Coleman's nursery at the High Road end of Church Road. The factory employed 140 people before Herbert retired in 1837, and was then taken over by crêpe manufacturers until it was destroyed by fire in 1860.

In 1815 Louis Frebout opened a silk-winding factory in what became known as Factory Lane, just off the High Road. By 1820 it had become a lace-making factory with some 300 employees, and in 1837 it changed again when it was taken over by the London Caoutchouc Company. Warne's rubber factory, as it later became known, expanded steadily and was an important local employer. The fire of 1839 (described by Albert Hill, above) destroyed one

106　*Williamson's Pottery Works, Green Lanes, in 1895.*

of its four-storey buildings, but the factory did not close. It was extended to include a 160 ft high stack, a notable landmark. In 1904 part of the site was sacrificed for the development of Dowsett Road, but it continued to produce rubber solution and sundry articles until the First World War.

Brewing was another significant local industry, using the good water supplies, and there were several breweries in the area. The extensive Bell Brewery in the High Road, owned by the Gripper family in 1862, was taken over by Whitbread in 1896 and turned to a bottling plant. The breweries were closed by 1924 and demolished in 1927. The days of warm beer were numbered when a German company established the Tottenham Lager Beer Brewery and Ice Factory at the former Grove House school. Managed by Otto Vollman in 1890, this huge brewery continued until 1936, when the buildings became a cold store.

During the 19th century these factories and breweries were joined by printers, coach builders, piano makers and many other small trades and workshops, but from the early part of the 20th century large and nationally important industries were established in Tottenham. In 1900 Harris Lebus opened his furniture works on fields by the Lea close to Tottenham Hale. Lebus was the son of a Jewish immigrant from Germany who set up a furniture workshop in Whitechapel in

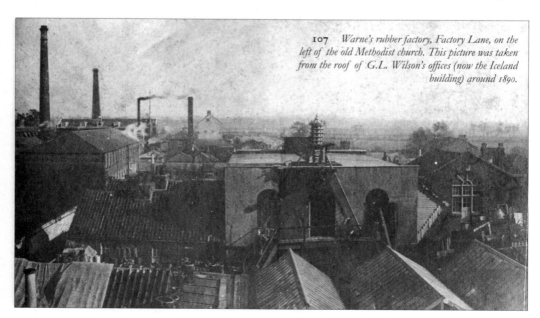

107　*Warne's rubber factory, Factory Lane, on the left of the old Methodist church. This picture was taken from the roof of G.L. Wilson's offices (now the Iceland building) around 1890.*

the firm left Tottenham in 1969. One part of the site has become a large housing estate; the other part was for many years the Greater London Council depot but it has recently also become a housing estate.

Another factory to move out of the East End to Tottenham Hale had an important impact on the growth of office work. In 1906 David Gestetner, also a Jewish immigrant, opened his works in Broad Lane where he produced the rotary duplicating machine, using silk-screen mounted stencils for typewriters. Gestetner invented his equipment as a quick and efficient copying process of great value to the burgeoning office world, and the firm continued to develop and refine copying processes to become first a national and then a multi-national company, expanding into many different aspects of office equipment. By the 1980s the Tottenham factories, still producing ink duplicators, had been overtaken by the introduction of photocopying and had to close.

Other office equipment firms were established in the Hale area. The stationers company Millingtons and Sons were established in Fountayne Road in 1903, later merging with John Dickinson in 1918. Nearby in Ashley Road was the Eagle Pencil Co., opened in 1907, which expanded steadily over the years, acquiring other pencil companies, and became Berol Limited by 1969. The firm moved out of Tottenham in 1992 but the building still stands, converted to offices and workshops.

In the north east of the parish was another important area of industrial development around Northumberland Park, where the engineer J.A. Prestwich had his works. Prestwich was a prolific inventor and manufacturer. In his first photographic equipment business, established in 1894, he helped develop the earliest cinematograph, but his main love was designing and making engines. He designed

108 *George Gripper of the successful Tottenham Brewing Company at the Bell Brewery in the High Road. Gripper was active in the local community and was the first chairman of Tottenham School Board.*

London's East End. The firm expanded under Harris, employing 1,000 workers, but there was no room to grow further. He then did what many Londoners have done, and moved out to Tottenham. Here there was space and transport, with a river delivering wood on barges and the railway taking the finished goods. The first building was completed by 1904 but over the years the factory expanded, eventually covering 40 acres by the Lea. Many of the workers in the early years were Jewish migrants from Europe who settled in the crowded streets around Tottenham Hale, where for a time they were regarded as an alien community, sometimes referred to as 'Little Russia'. Lebus, one of the largest furniture factories in the world, went on to become a significant local employer until

109   *The Lebus factory, established in 1904, expanded rapidly to cover, eventually, 40 acres by the River Lea. It made furniture such as this 1930s walnut bedroom suite.*

some early motor cars and became interested in aeroplanes, making the engine for the first historic flight of A.V. Roe in 1909. He also designed and made his own monoplane, which was flown over the marshes by his partner H.J. Harding.

But J.A.P.'s main specialisation was motor cycles, and the first works were opened at 1a Lansdowne Road in 1903. The products were commercially successful and by 1911 Prestwich transferred to a considerably larger plant in Northumberland Park, where his motorcycle engines, munitions and aircraft parts were particularly in demand with the outbreak of the First World War. In spite of the popularity of his new racing engine after the war, the firm experienced difficult times until the launch of a new engine in the 1930s. This portable industrial petrol engine was reliable and could be adapted for many uses, here and overseas, including powering tractors, pumping water, generating electricity and driving machinery. The company was able to produce 240,000 units

for the Second World War effort, as well as manufacture munitions and other equipment. J.A.P. continued to prosper after the war, but overseas competition led to the closure of the factory in 1963.

BUYING AND SELLING

As Tottenham grew, so did the number and variety of shops spreading either side of the High Road, often replacing the large old houses and making their way up other main thoroughfares. All the newly built streets had their corner shops – the grocers, butchers, sweetshop or dairy – and even inconspicuous side streets would have a row of shops. In 1907, Poynton Road on the Coleraine estate boasted a beer shop, baker, fishmonger, grocer, post office, greengrocer, boot mender and oil and colour shop (general hardware). With no refrigerators, daily shopping, small shops and low turnovers were the order of the day. Many of the shops also made local deliveries, particularly dairies, which went out three times with milk churns to ladle out milk into the customers own containers.

By the beginning of the 20th century, larger and more exciting places, offering more choice, were making their appearance. Groceries could be bought from the new chain stores opening along the High Road, such as Liptons, Home and Colonial and Sainsbury's. Opened in the High Road near the police station around 1903, Sainsbury's soon became a popular and reliable store, noted for its quality produce and range of own brand goods. With its marble counters, mosaic floors and assistants in white aprons, this was clearly a quality establishment. Customers queued at the long counters to watch the assistants neatly slice ham, cut cheese, weigh out sugar and tea into paper bags, and shape the half pounds of butter with their long wooden pats.

Other shops along the High Road were a mixture of old and new. Some large houses were converted into shops, such as Henderson's at numbers 692-4 selling seeds, plants and flowers. The family lived on the premises and used the grounds behind the house as a plant nursery. Other large houses were pulled down to make way for modern parades of shops, such as Criterion Buildings near Lansdowne Road and Windsor Parade between Reform Row and Dowsett Road. The old coaching inns had not yet been squeezed out by these new arrivals and their role in supplying travellers continued. Alongside the smart new shops opposite Bruce Grove station, the *George and Vulture*'s farrier continued to work until after the First World War.

West Green Road also had a remarkable range of commerce and the street was usually busy throughout the day. Shops stayed open late, particularly on Saturdays, the pavements being lit in the dark winter evenings by the large gas lamps hanging outside. They attracted poorer shoppers seeking a bargain when meat had to be sold off, or workers on their way home. The

110   *In 1906 David Gestetner opened his works in Broad Lane manufacturing the rotary duplicating machine. The machine enabled offices to produce copies of documents quickly and efficiently and was a significant part of all offices until the photocopier took over in the 1980s.*

display of goods in the window of Matthews Bros at no. 96 attracted many of Tottenham's new consumers. The shop sold bikes and a wide range of sports equipment, and its advertising boasted that 'For ease, comfort and durability,

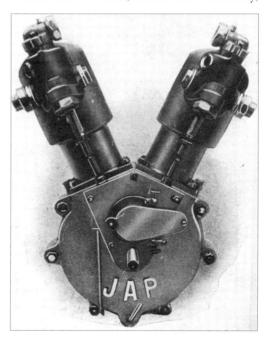

111   *J.A. Prestwich's water-cooled twin-cylinder 6hp engine.*

ride Goodwin's Cycles … A marvel of cheapness, made only by Matthews Bros., at their steam works'. Matthews provided and mended bikes for local cyclists.

One particularly exciting store was the Marks & Spencer Penny Bazaar in West Green Road, its 'free admission' encouraging browsers as well as shoppers. It opened in 1905, and by 1916 had been joined by another store in the High Road opposite Bruce Grove station. The Bruce Grove store spread out in the following years to take over the other shops in the parade, whilst the little shop in West Green closed in 1936. After many successful decades, the store eventually closed in the 1970s following the retrenchment caused by larger shopping centres, and the premises are now a McDonalds.

Another interesting shopping development at the turn of the century took place in the High Road between West Green Road and Seven Sisters. A parade of shops owned by the Ward family sold furniture, household furnishings and jewellery. Around the corner at no. 11 West

112   *Woman assistant in Taylor's bakery, Church Road, photographed by William Atkinson in 1911. Small baker's such as this provided freshly baked bread in a number of local side streets.*

Green Road was another thriving Ward's store selling clothing. These eventually amalgamated into a department store, and from the 1920s Ward's Stores was a very popular shop with a reputation across north-east London and a wide variety of goods under one roof. It had an unusual centralised cashier system, probably to ensure there was no fraud by either customers

114 *Marks & Spencer Penny Bazaar in West Green Road, c.1907*

or staff. When goods were paid for, the money was put into a cylindrical container which was whirled away along overhead wires to the cashiers' office. After a while the container arrived back to the counter with the customer's receipt and change.

113 *Shops owned by the Ward family on the High Road between Seven Sisters and West Green Road, c.1905. These were later merged to become Tottenham's first department store.*

In 1921 Ward's was joined by Tottenham's second department store, Burgess's in the High Road, on the site of the old Sanchez almshouses. With its plate-glass, island-style windows, arcades and spacious layout, it offered an enjoyable browsing experience, as well as a wide range of goods. Both stores were established by local businessman, but a third department store opened in 1930, the Co-operative, which was part of the wider Co-operative movement. It sold clothes and furniture as well as food, and offered its customers the benefit of the 'divi', paid on profits to Co-op members.

In the 1980s the Co-op moved to Burgess's premises, but not for long. The handsome

115   *Rectory Farm on White Hart Lane, c.1900, when it was still possible to find rural sights such as this in parts of the largely urbanised parish*

building, Sanchez House, came down to be replaced by a supermarket and offices. The former Co-op building has been preserved as a carpet store with housing above. Ward's, closed in 1972 and partly ravaged by fire, has reverted to small shops and an indoor market, but this part of the High Road is still known as Ward's Corner.

FARMS AND GARDENS

Agriculture declined rapidly as housing and industry grew. Most farmers were tenants, and their absentee landlords, looking for profit, were happy to sell the land off for development. But at the beginning of the century there were still a few farms, market gardens and nurseries. In the west of the parish Devonshire Hill farm, off Devonshire Hill Lane, spread across Tottenham and Wood Green. It produced mixed crops, probably for local consumption, along with cows, pigs, chickens and hay meadows. By

1910 the fields off Devonshire Hill Lane had been acquired by the adjoining Samuel South potteries to use as grazing for the firm's horses and hay for their winter feed. From 1921 horses gave way to motor vehicles, and the fields were used by sports clubs. Gradually they were sold off to be replaced by public buildings and amenities, as well as private and public housing.

A little further east along White Hart Lane was Rectory Farm, at one time the home farm of the Rectory Manor estate. The main farm was opposite Rectory House (later part of the cemetery), but there were fields and an older farmhouse in the Wood Green parish which were acquired by the pottery firm, E.G. Cole, in 1922. Most of the main farm was sold to Tottenham Urban District Council in 1920 for housing development, and the farmhouse and yard in 1935 for private housing.

Broadwaters farm on Lordship Lane was occupied by Mr Andrews at the turn of the century. These fields were traditionally known as Broadwaters from the regular flooding of the nearby Moselle, which created rich meadowland for cattle. Andrews delivered his milk directly to the local market, but by 1916 the farm had ceased to operate. The land was acquired by Tottenham UDC and later became Lordship Recreation Ground, although some was used for allotments until the building of the Broadwater Farm Estate in the 1960s. Asplins, one of the oldest farms in Tottenham, continued farming as late as 1933. Located on the edge of the marshes at the eastern end of Marsh Lane, it was cut off from the encroaching streets by the railway line. But not always from the local children, who would occasionally take the opportunity to lift a carrot or two.

Tottenham's agriculture was small scale and mainly arable, producing root crops, vegetables, milk, poultry and meat largely for the local market. In previous centuries it extended to sending hay or fattened cattle to London, and this trade now gave rise to the more commercial practice of market gardening, nurseries and flower production. As far back as the 17th century small fields had been given over to growing roses, either for perfume or cut flowers. In the 18th century William Coleman established his successful market garden on land either side of Church Road, with more acres south of Marsh Lane. Most of the nurseries were auctioned off in 1810 after Coleman's death, and in 1833 the remaining land in Church Road was sold to lace manufacturer Mr Herbert. The nurseries were a significant concern in Tottenham at one time, and are now remembered by the name of Nursery Street off Church Road.

116 *Broadwaters Farm in Lordship Lane was still clinging on up until the First World War but, located in the centre of Tottenham, with housing going up around it, it had ceased to operate by 1916.*

117 *Henderson's the seed merchants in the High Road, c.1909. They had a nursery behind the shop, as well as ones in Scotland Green and along Marsh Lane at a time when market gardening was a thriving industry in Tottenham.*

Market gardening was a greater commercial concern further up the Lea Valley, but a number of successful nurseries in Tottenham specialised in plants, flowers and seeds. During the latter years of the 19th century, the Henderson family had nurseries in Scotland Green (Kemble Nursery) and Marsh Lane (White House Nursery), and later opened their seed shop, with nursery garden, in the High Road. Many nurserymen now used greenhouses to produce flowers and fruits for Covent Garden and the London market as well as the general public, but they could still be vulnerable to the weather. In 1876 a violent thunderstorm caused extensive damage to greenhouses and the forced flowers and fruits in them. One of the largest growers, Rochfords of Page Green, estimated over £1,000 of damage, including vines that would take 'one or two seasons before they could recover'. Mr Howell of Clyde Road stated quite simply that he had 'lost his all'.

There were many commercial nurserymen in the area around Tottenham Hale where good growing land was available, and convenient rail transport provided swifter delivery to the London markets. The most successful nurseryman was Thomas Ware of Hale Farm nursery, who specialised in bulbs and plants for people's gardens as well as flowers for Covent Garden. His nursery was taken over in the 1890s by Francis Fell, but in 1900 Fell was compelled to move the nurseries to Feltham, Middlesex, 'owing to the very extensive building operations and railway developments' on the old site. The mean streets were encroaching, and although a few nurseries carried on until after the First World War, particularly in and around the marshes, even these had faded away by the time of the Second World War.

ELEVEN

Out and About

Although housing and industry were taking over Tottenham's last fields, and the area was described by one commentator in 1909 as 'a mass of mean streets, truly awful in their monotony', there were still plenty of opportunities for enjoyment, both indoors and out. There continued to be places for walking and roaming, for children, adults and families. Lanes led through fields and farms west of Lordship Lane to White Hart Lane, and onwards to Enfield. In the east of the parish the fields by the Lea were still open. One resident recalled the crowds on Sundays, some of whom enjoyed the pleasure boats on the river. For a special day out, such as a Bank Holiday, families could visit the pleasure gardens of the *Ferry Boat Inn* and enjoy Day's Dancing Ground with its brass band, and the fairs and swings on nearby fields.

Children in particular relished these open spaces. One resident remembered the marshes when she was a girl: 'We would take a bottle of water or lemonade, and some sandwiches – we had jam or dripping – and go and spend a day there. It used to be lovely. And in the summer we used to play over the hayfields and make hay huts … there used to be piles of hay.' The boys were sometimes more adventurous, walking across the marshes and onwards to Chingford and Epping Forest.

PARKS AND COMMONS

For several decades open land was saved from building development by the actions of the local Council, often after campaigning from local residents. It bought up the extensive grounds of some the big old houses after their owners left the area and turned them into parks. The first park, bought in 1892, was Bruce Castle, an attractive open space containing the community's oldest and most famous house. The landscaped park had a pond and fountain donated in 1893 by the British Women's Temperance Association to encourage water drinking rather than ale. Both the pond and fountain have gone, but a children's playground, bowling green and tennis courts have been added.

Bruce Castle was closely followed by Chestnuts in 1898 and Downhills Park in 1902. Later, in 1932, the Lordship Lane recreation ground opened on the site of Broadwaters Farm. Running from Downhills Park through to Lordship Lane, the parks made a continuous green space through the centre of Tottenham. The Townsend Trustees, who owned the last of the manor land, also gifted 43 acres to the Council, including the last commons of Tottenham, West Green and Page Green.

The parks, and even the commons, were sometimes home to other attractions. Fairgrounds

118   *The drinking fountain in Bruce Castle park, opened in 1893, was paid for by donations from the British Women's Temperance Association to encourage water drinking instead of beer.*

became Down Lane recreation ground. Further south, the Markfield House grounds on the side of the Lea were bought by the Council in 1925 and opened as a park. Altogether the Council acquired some 160 acres of land during this period, which was preserved from housing and industry.

THE ACTIVE LIFE

The parks, marshes and private fields provided space for the more active, who shared the hay fields with a few remaining cattle. Fishing had long been popular on the Lea and was celebrated by Izaak Walton in *The Compleat Angler* of 1653; its popularity returned once better sewage disposal had led to cleaner waters. On freezing days in winter the waters could ice over and the more adventurous put on their skates, sometimes skating over the frozen flooded fields.

were frequent visitors and Sangers Circus had its winter headquarters by West Green common where there are now houses. They put up their big top and practised during the winter, setting off again in spring to tour the country. They formed a long parade, dressed in their circus finery and with riders on horseback, and West Green Road was lined from the common to Turnpike Lane with residents enjoying the free display.

In the east, the Lammas land on the marshes was invested in the Council following the 1900 Act, and in 1905 a further 25 acres of the marshes was acquired from the Metropolitan Water Board, together with the Down field, which

For summer days there was the open-air swimming pool built in 1905 on Clendish marsh close to Pymmes brook. Filled with water from the Lea, including some of its flora and fauna, this may have been for the more hardy swimmers, especially on colder days, but it provided an alternative to swimming in the river, or even the reservoirs – forbidden activities that were particularly attractive to young boys. The swimming pool remained open until the 1930s, when the more luxurious Lido was built by Lordship Recreation Ground.

A few wealthier gun-owning sportsmen went shooting over the reservoirs, and for the local volunteer militia there was shooting practice on the rifle butts. The militia was formed in 1859 and became the 33rd Middlesex (Tottenham) Volunteer Rifle Corps in 1860 and later the 3rd Middlesex Rifle Volunteers. The rifle range of 1,000 yards was opened in 1863 on the Wild Marsh, close to the Edmonton border, and was still in use at the beginning of the 20th century.

Many cricket, tennis, athletic and football clubs were established which used the parks and marshes for their games. Tottenham Cricket Club, based in Philip Lane by 1906, had started playing on the marshes. Its members were mainly local tradesmen and it was noted locally for its successful tour of Holland in 1890, playing four games and being 'easy winners' of three. Cycling had become a popular leisure activity from the end of the 19th century, after the

introduction of the safety cycle in 1885 and Dunlop's pneumatic tyres three years later made it a more comfortable and attainable activity, no matter how cumbersome the clothes of the time. Enthusiasts, including women, formed clubs and went on organised trips into the countryside. For the more athletic there was racing at venues such as the Wood Green Cycling Track.

THE BEAUTIFUL GAME

Another cricket team went on to become better known as a football club. The club was formed in 1882 by cricketers who wanted to continue to meet over the winter months, so decided to play football. Two years later it became the Tottenham Hotspur Football Club, with a notable local reputation and large crowds of spectators, attracting players from other clubs.

119 *Markfield Park in 1950, showing the flourishing gardens and flower beds.*

120   *Izaak Walton, who came to Tottenham to fish on the Lea, recorded his experience in* The Compleat Angler, *published in 1653.*

The team was named after Harry Hotspur of the Percy family, distantly related to Sir Hugh Smithson who lived at the Black House in the High Road in the 17th century, where Dial and Percy Houses are now. By 1889 the club had moved to an enclosed ground behind a meadow in Northumberland Park, but their last game on the marshes was their first against Woolwich Arsenal. The match was abandoned due to poor light, with 15 minutes to go and Spurs leading 2-1.

The Northumberland Park ground was shared with another football club and a tennis club, with ticketed entry and a stand. In 1899 Spurs moved to their present ground, White Hart Lane, taking their stand with them. They now had 2,500 seats under cover, parking for bikes and stabling for horses. The club turned professional in 1895, playing in the Southern and United Leagues. In 1901 Spurs became the only non-League side to win the FA Cup, defeating Sheffield United. At a time when northern teams and players were dominant in English football, they were also the first southern

121   *A fishing match at the Mill Stream, Tottenham Hale, in 1875.*

club to win for 20 years. In 1908 they joined the Football League in Division Two, making it to Division One in their first season.

Even as an amateur team over the marshes, Spurs attracted several hundred spectators, and by the time they moved to Northumberland Park they were getting some 6,000 at the gate. Football had become a significant spectator sport in Tottenham, and in 1909 a Boxing Day match against Oldham attracted 40,000 people. The huge Saturday crowds making their way along Tottenham High Road, or by train to White Hart Lane station, became a familiar sight.

Few supporters could make it to the Cup Final replay at Bolton in 1901, but that night the High Road was packed with people until well after midnight waiting for the victorious team to arrive home. In compensation, films of the two matches were later shown at the football ground, projected on a large sheet in front of the grandstand. Tottenham brass band attended and there was music, singing and dancing – and a chance to view the cup.

A FEW INDOOR AMUSEMENTS

During the 19th century various clubs and societies were set up, some for intellectual stimulation and others for entertainment and socialising. There were lecture halls, literary societies, social clubs and music groups, as well as reading rooms and lending libraries. Local halls put on penny readings, magic lantern slides, concerts and dramatic performances. At the Lordship Lane Social Gathering male members met for lectures and discussions. In 1880 members agreed 'that ladies be invited to attend meetings that are thought desirable'.

These were largely serious and earnest activities, dominated by the middle class, but a more light-hearted entertainment was beginning to emerge that was attractive to all classes. The music hall, which had its origin in public houses, emerged as a mass entertainment in the late 19th century. In 1901 the People's Palace of Varieties opened in a hall in Forster Road offering a bill of songs, monologues, sketches and dramas. By 1907 a new, more glamorous, music hall

122 *The Rose and Crown Cricket Club prepare to play against Tottenham police on the Philip Lane cricket ground in 1890.*

123   *The White Hart running club in 1883. The club was based at the White Hart in Tottenham Hale.*

was being built nearby and the People's Palace turned to early cinema with Walturdaw's Electric Animated Pictures showing films twice nightly. The Tottenham Palace of Varieties opened in 1908 in the High Road opposite the police station. It was a handsome, comfortable and spacious building, designed by its architects Wylson and Long with safety very much in mind. The new Canadian Ice Rink opened alongside the Palace in 1909 on the corner site

124   *Tottenham Hotspur football team in the 1904-5 season.*

opposite the Drapers high school, but it seems the craze for skating was only temporary as we soon find the Canadian offering film shows.

The Palace also fell victim to changing fashions and by the 1920s was no longer attracting enthusiastic crowds. The last variety performance was in 1924. By 1925 the Canadian Cinema and Tottenham Palace, now under joint management, transformed themselves yet again to become the Palace Cinema and the Palais de Danse. The former skating rink had its greatest success as a dance hall, particularly in the sixties when, as the Tottenham Royal, its reputation spread across London and the suburbs. It ended life as a nightclub and was pulled down to make way for housing at the beginning of this century.

As it made its way through a succession of technological innovations, cinema became a particularly popular form of entertainment. The People's Palace in Forster Road and Canadian Cinema were joined by the Grand Picture House in the High Road by 1911, and the Corner Cinema on Seven Sisters Road and the

Imperial Cinema Theatre in West Green Road by 1913. The inter-war period was the heyday of cinema. Although the Forster Road and Canadian Cinemas disappear, they were replaced by the Bruce Grove Cinema and Dance Hall in 1921 and the Palace in 1925, then the Florida along the High Road by Lansdowne Road a little later. All have succumbed to declining audiences as television succeeded them in popularity. The Palace became a bingo hall in 1969, closing in the 1980s, and is now used by the Power Praise and Deliverance Ministries church. Other cinemas have been demolished to make way for offices or housing, although the Bruce Grove building is still there, serving as a snooker hall and church.

FURTHER AFIELD

By the 1930s more local people were venturing out of Tottenham, and indeed out of London, in their leisure time. Cycles, motorcycles and even cars enabled them to travel further afield. Other improvements in transport helped with this change. Train trips to seaside places such

125 *The Canadian Rink, c.1920, when it was the Electric Theatre cinema, with Tottenham Palace Variety Theatre behind.*

126   *The Corner Picture Theatre, c.1920, on the junction with Seven Sisters Road and the High Road. Ward's Stores can be seen on the right, with a smart horse and carriage waiting outside and an electric tram in the middle of the road, an interesting mix of class and transport.*

as Southend, Margate and Skegness were taken for the day, and local bus and coach companies, such as Ardleys, organised day trips or had regular routes out to Essex. Londoners had once come to Tottenham for outdoor leisure pursuits. Now Tottenham people were venturing even further in search of the disappearing countryside.

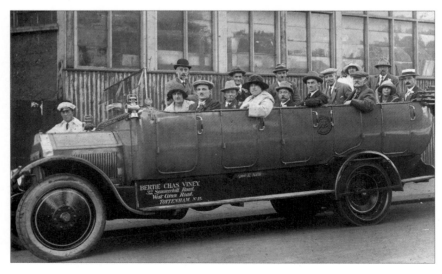

127   *Staff from G.L. Wilson, builder's merchants, on an annual outing in 1924. The motor brake was provided by Bertie Viney of Summerhill Road.*

TWELVE

Darker Times

When war was declared in 1914, Tottenham was prepared to play its part with enthusiasm. Volunteers enlisted, and local hospitals received the first wounded from the front. From the beginning war casualties were massive, and men on national reserve were called up. When volunteers were not enough, conscription was introduced in January 1916, whilst young boys and older men continued to be pressed to volunteer throughout the war.

In spite of popular sentiment and government commands, a few, such as the Quakers, resisted joining the fighting as a matter of conscience. But exemption on the grounds of conscientious objection was hard to obtain. Fred Murfin, who attended Tottenham Friends meetings but was not a Quaker, was sent to the front with other objectors where he refused to fight. His death sentence was only commuted to ten years imprisonment by the chance intervention of the British Minister of War.

Tottenham gave up its men, and its women took their place in the workforce in jobs previously barred to them, such as transport and heavy industry. They went to teach in boys' schools, and married teachers were asked to return, although such work had formerly been against local regulations. Women with families often had to work in factories after the death or injury of their husbands left them with little or no income, and the hours were long and exhausting. Tottenham's factories, such as J.A. Prestwich, Lebus and Gestetner, went over to producing munitions, and the work could be dangerous. A young girl of 18 was awarded an MBE for her courage in a fatal accident at work where she was very badly burnt. She later received pioneering 'artistic surgery' at the Prince of Wales for her facial burns and to save her sight.

The Prince of Wales and the Fever Hospital (St Ann's) took their share of the wounded from the front. Young women without family responsibilities became nurses doing stressful work, but they also took on additional responsibilities in the war effort. Like others in the community, they were trained to fire rifles for local defence should the anticipated invasion take place, and they helped till the land around the hospital for fruit and vegetables in order to ease the food shortages caused by the German blockades.

The early months of the war witnessed exceptional patriotic fervour, and this rebounded painfully on Tottenham's sizeable immigrant community from Germany and

128 *A military motorbike, part of the J.A. Prestwich wartime production. The gun could be used in different positions, including upwards when the gunner laid on the ground.*

Eastern Europe. Shops identified as being run by Germans, such as Smith's the jewellers on the Dowsett Road corner of the High Road, had their windows smashed, and people with foreign names hastily anglicised them.

One local teacher, Miss Kaiser, declared that she was now to be known as Miss King. German male civilians found themselves interned in Alexandra Palace from 1915, and many were deported after the war with their British-born families.

Patriotism continued throughout the war, with schools giving regular lessons on the Empire and the Navy, as well as organising savings stamps so children could contribute their pennies to the war effort. In November 1916 Tottenham schools were given a half-day holiday as a reward for subscribing £5,900 to the War Loan. As well as losing fathers, brothers and sons to the war, families at home had also to face bombing. Few bombs hit the town, but the sight of Zeppelins overhead brought fear and panic, and the one many local people saw being brought down over Cuffley would have been heartening. People sought shelter when there were raids, going

129 *The wrecked Zeppelin in Cuffley, September 1916. Airships such as this, loaded with bombs, frightened the civilian population. Although they did not cause local damage, they prepared residents for the severe bombing of the Second World War.*

130   *Peace celebrations in Love Lane, 1919. The children were given a cup and saucer and the men dressed in their old uniforms.*

131   *The London County Council Tower Gardens estate by Lordship Lane, c.1930, showing the central recreation ground set within the houses.*

to large buildings such as the Bell Brewery in the High Road or simply relying on the strength of their own passageways.

VICTORY AT A PRICE

The declaration of the Armistice on 11 November 1918 was greeted with joy and relief, followed by street parties, victory celebrations, parades and even medals for schoolchildren. But there was a darker side to the peace. Many men never returned, and some who came back were shattered and disabled, often unable to work again. One last blow to the exhausted population was influenza. This affected the young and healthy in particular and Tottenham was not immune. Bruce Castle was used as an emergency ward and schools were decimated by the illness. Some had to close for a week, and there were reports of deaths amongst pupils and teachers.

More problems were faced by returning soldiers looking for work. Some found their

132   *Culverting the Moselle brook, c.1907-10, for the LCC Peabody and Tottenham UDC council estates. The photograph is taken from the site of the later Risley Avenue, looking towards White Hart Lane.*

jobs gone with the downturn in trade, and others were unable to resume their old trades due to war injuries or nervous disabilities caused

133   *The opening of Devonshire Hill Library in 1935 by George Lansbury, MP, an active socialist and pacifist. Lansbury is in the front with local MP Bob Morrison on his right.*

134 *Robert, Fred and Alfred Rowley, c.1910. The Rowley brothers established a successful building firm, erecting many estates across Tottenham. The houses were rented out until sold, and the estate still owns many rented properties.*

by the trauma of combat. Working women, including war widows needing employment, had to give way to the returning men. The unemployment of the 1920s depression did not affect Tottenham as badly as northern towns, but it did have an impact and Tottenham formed its own branch of the National Unemployed Workers Movement. Local families took in the children of miners and the unemployed during times of particular hardship, including the miners' strike.

HOMES FIT FOR HEROES

Housing was the most acute need locally, as Tottenham's population rose to its peak of 157,772 in 1931. As many as a third of local families were known to be living in multi-occupation, with two families in houses that could barely contain one, sharing kitchens and toilets. Finding even this sort of accommodation was difficult and some families took to squatting. A group of ex-servicemen and their families took over Woodville Cottages in south Tottenham, but they must have been desperate as the properties were in a bad state of repair and the families were crowded into one room each. Private enterprise could not cope and, following the 1919 Housing Act, local councils, including Tottenham, took action to build homes. An earlier Act had enabled London County Council to buy land in 1901 on the north side of Lordship Lane and by 1914 the first wave of 954 houses (many of them with bathrooms) of the Tower Gardens estate had been built. The charitable Peabody Donation Fund had also built 154 cottages alongside this estate by 1907.

The two councils took over Tottenham's last remaining fields, from Lordship Lane to the Edmonton border, in order to create the Tower Gardens, White Hart Lane and Weir Hall estates. The LCC built homes for 10,000 tenants by 1938, and Tottenham over 800 between 1922 and 1928, with a further 300 in the 1930s. By 1926 the Devonshire Hill schools were opened to serve what had become a small town, and over the next decade the council built 25 shops along the Great Cambridge Road, as well as the Devonshire Hill library at Compton Crescent. Some of the building land had been Church property, part of the former Rectory Manor, and an acre was kept back for a church between Laburnum and Acacia Roads. At first a small mission hall, St Hilda's, was built, then the foundation of St John the Baptist, fronting White Hart Lane, was laid in 1939. In 1934 the Catholic chapel of St Bede was established in Compton Crescent.

Private housing filled the spaces left along White Hart Lane, as well as the remaining gaps east of the High Road and around Dowsett Road. Many of the Dowsett estate houses were erected by successful building firm Rowleys to a standard 1930s style, a pattern that served them well across Tottenham. Meanwhile, old and inadequate housing was being tackled through slum clearance. The courts and alleys of Scotland Green were cleared and replaced by new houses, completed in 1941, although further clearance and rebuilding was interrupted by the outbreak of another war in 1939.

LOOKING FORWARD

In 1934 Tottenham UDC became a municipal borough. By this time there had been a number of new developments: the Shell open-air theatre for dancing, music and drama opened in Lordship Recreation Ground in 1936, and the Lido outdoor swimming pool which opened a year later beside the park was a far cry from the old pool on the marshes. With a large pool and diving boards, a paddling pool, sunbathing

135 *The lido open-air swimming pool on Lordship Lane, shown here soon after it opened in 1937, was a popular attraction during the summer months.*

136 *Children practise their speaking and listening skills for shopping at Blanche Nevile School for the Deaf, c.1946.*

areas and a cafeteria, it was a popular place for visitors of all ages and ideally situated near the new estates. Sunny days saw long queues on the concourse outside, but bad weather limited visits, and the Lido was closed in the 1980s as uneconomic. The site has since been used for housing, and nearby Rowland Hill secondary modern school, built in 1938 has also since been redeveloped for housing. On the other side of the park, former farmland was used for allotments until the 1960s, when these made way for the Broadwater Farm estate.

More was being done to address the needs of Tottenham's children, particularly in relation to health and education. A clinic built in Park Lane opened in time to meet the urgent needs of war. It included a nursery for babies, as well as clinics for teeth, sight and child development. Two special schools had opened by 1928 for children with disabilities. The oldest, Blanche Nevile School for the Deaf, had started in 1895 at the Cedars but by 1924 was housed in newly built accommodation in Philip Lane. In 1928 the Vale School for children with physical handicaps or heart trouble opened in Vale Road, south Tottenham, where Tottenham's first nursery school was also built in 1937.

Attempts were being made to extend secondary education to all. Government initiatives had foundered on economic instability, but Tottenham Council made its own improvements following the 1918 Education Act with the establishment of three selective central schools, Down Lane, Downhills and Risley. The schools took pupils from 11 to 15 years, and provided a largely commercial and technical curriculum, although academic subjects were taught at

Friday, Sept. 15th, 1939.

TOTTENHAM & EDMONTON WEEKLY HERALD.

TOTTENHAM'S EVACUATED CHILDREN

THEY'RE HAVING A WONDERFUL TIME

Foster Parents' Generous Welcome

They are washing for the children, cooking and mending for them, even providing clothing for the ill-equipped, even buying comic papers for them.

137   *A report in the* Tottenham Herald *of September 1939 offered encouraging news for the parents of evacuees, presenting the experience as one of kindness and country pleasures.*

138   *Evacuees from Woodlands Park school, c.1940, helping on a farm in Huntingdon.*

a level approaching the grammar schools. A similar education could be obtained in the County Council Technical College. Originally founded in 1892 in the old Grove House school, by the mid 1930s it had been rebuilt and housed three departments: a junior technical school for boys aged 13 to 16, a mixed commercial school for the same ages, and evening classes catering for up to 1,400 students.

Although the school leaving age remained at 14, from 1934 the Council started to reorganise elementary schools and create separate secondary schools from age 11. Eight schools were established, some mixed and some single sex, and for three years pupils were given a more specialised subject education. But the intervention of the war prevented the school leaving age being raised to provide a more respectable four-year secondary education.

WAR RETURNS

When the Second World War was declared, on 3 September 1939, Tottenham was prepared. Schools re-opened early on 26 August to become evacuation centres for children. Severe bombing was anticipated and plans had been developed over a number of months to remove children and mothers with babies to safer places in the country. On 1 September children assembled in school halls with their gas masks and labels, their cases and knapsacks packed with what was all too often inadequate clothing. They said goodbye to their mothers and set off with their teachers to the nearest train station, no one knowing their destination. Secrecy was deemed the order of the day.

They went to villages in Essex, Cambridgeshire, Suffolk and Hertfordshire, arriving tired, hungry and thirsty after their long journeys. They were billeted on local families through a process of selection, distressing for the child picked last, or those who did not want to be separated from siblings. Some families took the children willingly, others didn't, and the children had varying experiences in their strange new homes. A few enjoyed the pleasures of country life and others settled in well with welcoming families. Some had more miserable experiences, with homesickness or unfriendly treatment and neglect and, not unusually, the embarrassment of bed wetting. One girl remembers attempting to run away with her sister to get back to her family, although the people they were with had been very kind.

A deliberately reassuring report in the *Tottenham and Edmonton Weekly Herald* of 15 September painted a picture of happy children free to wander the 'wide green fields' and play in rivers, streams and pools, looked after with 'care and affection' by their foster families. The report also noted the need to replace inadequate or absent nightwear, slippers and underwear for many of the poorer children. One reason for roaming the wide green fields was the lack of available school accommodation during the first few weeks. Fortunately the weather was exceptionally sunny, and one Coleraine teacher remembered keeping the children occupied for the first two weeks with walking and nature study. After that accommodation was found in a tiny hall, but education was still part-time as children were taught on a shift basis.

Although the draconian evacuation methods give the impression of compulsion, families could choose whether to send their children away. The Gates family of Seymour Avenue did not want to be split up and stayed in Tottenham to take their chances with the bombing and at least 'die together'. Over the first few months of the war they were joined by numbers of returning evacuees when the anticipated bombing failed to materialise and families and children realised they did not have to continue to endure the miseries of separation.

But in September 1940 the 'blitzkrieg' started. The country was subjected to eight months of intensive bombing and Tottenham, just north of London, did not escape. Again the town was prepared, air-raid shelters having already been distributed by one of the first authorities in the country to do so. Anderson shelters erected in dugouts in the garden or sturdy indoor Morrison shelters served many as a refuge at home, whilst others went to the large trench shelters made in areas of open ground such as parks and commons. The shelters undoubtedly saved lives, but were not themselves immune to a direct hit. A bomb that hit the Downhills shelter in Lordship Recreation Ground is reported to have killed some 150 people.

The blitz lasted until May 1941, but bombing continued throughout the war with destructive landmines and incendiaries that would cause widespread damage if the blazes were not stopped. Towards the end of the war the deadly menace of the remote controlled V1 and V2 rockets, with their sudden and unpredictable explosions, continued to terrify civilians. The last V2 rocket to fall on Tottenham just missed the grammar school in White Hart Lane, where some 400 pupils were at their desks, but its destructive power was such that the building was damaged and two boys, Peter Goodman and Harold Poulton, died and another was badly injured.

Compulsory blackout at night time was instituted to avoid detection by enemy planes, adding to the miseries of bombing. The civil defence organised warden patrols and fire watchers, and air-raid sirens sounded whenever enemy planes were spotted. The fire service was on constant call throughout and the Auxiliary Fire Service tackled small-scale fires from incendiary bombs. Civilian life was strained to the utmost. Schools remained closed until air-raid shelters had been installed and started gradually re-opening from the beginning of 1940, first on a part-time basis. Teachers returned from evacuation and

139   *Back gardens of houses along the railway between Seven Sisters and Bruce Grove, c.1940, showing the hump of the Anderson shelter bottom right.*

140   *Tewkesbury Road in south Tottenham was badly damaged by bombing and the houses were later removed during the rebuilding of the Tiverton estate.*

learned to cope with lessons disrupted by air raids and the effect on staff and pupils of consequent wakeful nights. Teachers, like other adults with full-time jobs, were also engaged in civil defence duties at night such as fire watching.

Increasingly the schools were seen as a place to keep children secure and occupied whilst their mothers went to work in place of the men who had gone to fight. Holiday play centres were established, free milk was provided and school meals were made available to all, instead of the poorer few who received them before the war. Sometimes these were served in the nearby British Restaurants, catering for adults as well as children. Cookery lessons for older girls were specifically aimed at producing cheap and nutritious meals within the constraints of food shortages, and parents were invited to an open day to pick up advice and hints.

The need to ensure people ate healthily in the face of considerable food shortages was a key part of government policy. Rationing was introduced to ensure an equitable distribution

141   *Inside the civil defence control centre in 1945, located in the reasonable safety of the basement of the Polytechnic.*

of basic food items, allotments were dug on all available pieces of land, and gardens utilised for vegetables. The borough introduced its famous 'Tottenham pudding' of food scraps collected and recycled for the local piggeries. The refuse depot in Park Lane received the waste and boiled it down for pigs kept on site as well as at other locations such as a corner of Tottenham Cemetery. The King's mother, Queen Mary, came to inspect the process and the piggery in August 1940. The waste collection lasted into the 1950s, and many residents can recall the pungent smell of the 'pig bins', as the waste containers were called.

Anything that could be was recycled: clothes, paper, glass and metal. Imports were badly affected by the blockades and factories were hungry for raw material, especially those producing for the war effort. Once again factories such as Lebus, Gestetner's and JAP turned to war production, and again women were employed in men's jobs. These now included driving ambulances during bombing raids, as well as joining the Land Army. The Women's Volunteer Service organised salvage collections, savings, meal services, mobile canteens and many of the other wartime activities.

AN EXHAUSTED PEACE

When Victory in Europe was announced in May 1945 there were ecstatic celebrations. Many Tottenham residents joined the celebrating crowds in Trafalgar Square, and street parties were organised across the town. Dancing returned to the Tottenham Royal, with the added attraction of visiting American soldiers and airmen. But the joy was tempered with the knowledge of the numbers of people who had lost their lives, as well as those still engaged in fighting in the Far East. The Garden of Remembrance was opened in Tottenham Cemetery in 1952, to join the War Memorial erected on Tottenham Green in 1923 after the First War, and a marble wall commemorates the civilian and armed dead.

142   *Queen Mary, with various local dignitaries in August 1940, inspects the casts of Tottenham Pudding, which used waste food for feeding to pigs in the council piggeries.*

143   *Members of the Women's Volunteer Service using the central library to sort items for recycling and for people bombed out of their homes.*

144   *Victory celebrations in 1945 at a street party in Ranelagh Road.*

145   *The consecration and opening of the Garden of Remembrance in Tottenham Cemetery in 1952.*

Thirteen

Looking Back

In 1965 Tottenham became part of the London Borough of Haringey and was finally submerged into the city. The 20 years following the war had been years of privation, followed by consolidation and improvements, with further drastic developments after 1965.

POPULAR PREFABS

Like many areas of the country, Tottenham faced housing shortages arising from bomb damage, whilst the pre-war problems of overcrowding and slums had not gone away. The emergency response was to erect bungalows made from parts prefabricated in factories that could rapidly replace houses destroyed or badly damaged during the war. Fifty-eight sites were identified for the prefabs, mainly very small plots, mostly located around White Hart Lane. By 1946 some 256 homes had been completed, although with 6,630 applications demand far outstretched supply. The well-designed houses, with their wooden floors, kitchens and bathrooms, were very popular and families did not want to leave them when the time came to move to new homes. They were lovingly furnished with 'utility' furniture, such as that produced by Lebus in the post-war years. Rationing did not end with the war, and the years following saw continuing shortages in food, clothing and consumer goods.

The Council had requisitioned property for people bombed out of their homes, and it retained nearly 2,000 family units in 1955. Plans were made to rebuild in war-damaged Asplins, Manor and Chalgrove roads, and land was purchased in Potters Bar for an estate of 300 homes. But there was now little open land left for building on, apart from pockets at White Hart Lane and Northumberland Park and alongside Lordship Recreation Ground.

Most of the building land came from slum clearance. Tewkesbury Road in south Tottenham disappeared and the Tiverton estate was built by Seven Sisters Road. The old houses along High Cross, Chesnut, Colsterworth, Welbourne and Somerset roads were demolished and the Chesnuts estate erected. In north Tottenham, the notorious Lorenco Road and Love Lane were pulled down, as well as Wagon Lane on the other side of the High Road, the old, closely packed streets replaced by tower blocks leavened by a few low-rise buildings. More substantial, middle-class, housing was not immune either, and many of the villas built along Northumberland Park during the 1850s gave way to the modern housing estate from the 1950s.

Although every available piece of land was utilised to build more houses, the overwhelming pressure of numbers was easing. From a high of 157,772 in 1931, the population dropped to 126,929 in 1951 and 113,249 in 1961. Today, at nearly 100,000 in 2001, numbers are well below the level of the 1930s. Parks have been preserved, and matters never become so desperate that building had to take place on the marshes. There was even the chance to create a new green space when Hartington Park was opened in the 1970s where once there had been streets of old Victorian houses, shops and workshops alongside the Carbuncle stream.

146 *Two types of prefab were built, one in a bungalow style, shown here between High Cross and Tottenham Hale, and the other in a rounded shape, rather similar to the Anderson shelters. They were built between 1945 and 1950.*

IN WITH THE NEW

Once the worst of the food, housing and commodities shortages were over, life began to improve. Schools re-established full staffing following an intensive national teacher training programme, and from 1946 the last of the all-age elementary schools closed. Schools were now reorganised into infants and juniors for primary children, and grammar, central and secondary modern schools for the over-elevens. In 1967 a further reorganisation of secondary schools introduced the comprehensive system, with Drayton School (now Gladesmore) replacing Markfield School in South Tottenham, and

Northumberland Park opening in 1972 in South Tottenham.

From 1970 to 1972 primary schools were built on the new housing estates at Tiverton, Welbourne and Broadwater Farm. Two special schools were opened on Broadwater Farm in 1970, Moselle school, for children with learning difficulties, and William C. Harvey, for more serious and profound difficulties, provided a quality education for children who had previously been deemed unfit to learn. Two nursery schools, Pembury House in Lansdowne Road and Rowland Hill in White Hart Lane, were opened during the war, and have continued

147 *Inside a prefab with a curved roof. The view from the living room shows two bedrooms off, with a central fireplace. The kitchen and bathroom are behind the camera. It looks light, airy and well furnished, but such homes were replaced during the 1960s with modern housing.*

to flourish, although both schools have since been rebuilt.

In the 1950s rationing gradually ended, there was full employment and the housing situation began to improve. The High Road shops were thriving, as well as the cinemas and dance halls. The traffic along the main road had been eased a little by the building of the Great Cambridge road in the 1930s, which took the A10 up Bruce Grove, through the LCC estate and on to Edmonton, but motor traffic continued to increase. By 1969 the newly built Victoria line had provided Tottenham with long-awaited access to the 'tube', with stations at Seven Sisters and Tottenham Hale. The Hale went on to become a modern version of the transport interchange that it had been in the Middle Ages, with over and underground railways replacing the river, and a new highway, Monument Way, replacing the old High Cross Road.

OUT WITH THE OLD

As a result of the housing and industrial developments, as well as the changing tastes of the modern consumer, many old landmarks went by the wayside. Most of the grand old houses disappeared, along with the farms and open spaces. Cinemas and dancehalls were replaced by housing

and churches, and the old coaching inns which lasted well into the 20th century as public houses have also disappeared. The *Bull, George and Vulture, Plough, Rose and Crown, Roe Buck,* and *Wagon and Horses* have been closed and demolished. The *Swan,* for so long a landmark on the corner of Philip Lane, has recently closed and awaits its fate, and other large public houses, such as the *Red Lion,* a 17th-century coaching inn by Lansdowne Road, and the *Prince of Wales* on Scotland Green have gone. Survivors on the High Road include the *Ship Inn* by Bruce Grove, given a more modern image, and the *Bell and Hare* by Park Lane, built on charity land, which continues to flourish. The *Ferry Boat Inn* on Ferry Lane is also with us, and its gardens by the river and restaurant are reminiscent of the earlier Tudor coaching inns.

In the 1960s once thriving shops started to face serious competition from shopping centres such as Wood Green, and one by one the chain stores and the independent department stores left the area. Many small independent shops have appeared in their place, catering for a more diverse community as Tottenham's population has undergone further dramatic change. It is now home to people from across the world, and their impact is shown by the new shops, cafes and places of worship. In the schools, nearly

148 *Cottage Place, Broad Lane, between the Hale and Hale Gardens, 1907. These very old cottages (possibly 17th-century) have been replaced by the Tottenham Hale gyratory system and the new housing estates.*

149   *A rebuilt* Tottenham Swan *in 1920. This very old established inn, mentioned by Izaak Walton, still looks like this today, rather shabbier than in this picture. It has now closed.*

150   *The* Ferry Boat Inn *on Ferry Lane in a quiet, rural scene around 1900, with a carriage horse having a rest and meal break. Today this same inn is alongside the busy Ferry Lane to Walthamstow, although its riverside position can take us back to earlier days.*

three-quarters of the children are from ethnic minorities, speaking around 190 languages between them.

STILL WITH US

Some old buildings and places are with us still, even if their use and surroundings have changed. The Grade 1 listed Bruce Castle building has survived many difficult times, particularly in the 1950s when substantial repairs were needed, but is now a handsome relic of this ancient inhabited area. Across Church Lane, the old parish church of All Hallows has experienced frequent repair and rebuilding since its original foundation around the 11th century, and is a mixture of many periods. The tower remains the oldest part and the south porch, with its first-floor chantry chapel, dates back to the 16th century. In 1875 the architect William Butterfield contributed to renovations of the church, including the chancel and the removal of Lord Coleraine's vestry. Butterfield is buried in Tottenham Cemetery.

Alongside the church is the Priory, once thought to be the residence of the priors of Holy Trinity. It was built in 1620 for Joseph Fenton, replacing the original farmhouse. The Priory was saved from demolition by the Rev. Denton Jones in 1906, when he moved there from the former vicarage at 776 High Road, bringing the wrought-iron gates with him. Alongside the Priory is Parkside Preparatory school, the early 19th-century home of Albert Hill, of the Hill family of Bruce Castle school, which was then called Prioryside.

The nearby cemetery is an unexpected oasis of green, particularly the Garden of Remembrance by White Hart Lane. The grand old Parsonage, later the Rectory House, was demolished in 1904, but most of the grounds were used for this part of the cemetery, where a lovely lake attracts water birds and the Moselle stream can still be seen in its unculverted state. Opposite the cemetery, just off Church Lane, are the listed houses of Prospect Place, built in 1822 and still retaining an air of quiet rural seclusion.

Close to Bruce Castle, in Bruce Grove, are the old Almshouses built in 1868 around a pleasant green and with their own chapel. They were built by three City foundations as part of the move out to more rural surroundings. Originally known as the Drapers, the almshouses today are called Edmonsons and, following substantial renovation, are still in use as homes for the elderly. Towards the High Road end of Bruce Grove are the handsome semi-detached houses built between 1785 and 1820, mainly for local Quaker families. Each pair is individually designed, and all have now been converted to flats and commercial accommodation, although some, including Luke Howard's former home at No. 7, are in a state of dilapidation.

At the north end of the High Road, near White Hart Lane, is a notable cluster of old houses flanking the Spurs ground. Northumberland Terrace, Nos 794-782 High Road, was built between 1750-2 on the site of the Black House. Nearby, at No. 796, is the late 17th-century Percy House; alongside is Dial House, its sundial on the side gable, dating from 1691. The pair of four-storey houses further along at 808-10 were built in the early 18th century. Round the corner in White Hart Lane, The Grange at Nos 32-4, built in the early 18th century, has been renovated and is now used as a Day Care Centre.

151 *The dining room of the Priory, Church Lane, c.1938. The plaque over the fireplace is an early one of Charles I, indicating the loyalties of former residents.*

Further south, opposite Park Lane, the early 18th-century Moselle House, named after the stream that ran close by until culverted, is not far from the Baptist Church built in 1825. Hawthorn Cottage of 1812, round the corner in King's Road, is a lonely survivor of older housing in James Place. By Scotland Green, the old Bluecoat school, built in 1833, has been refurbished and partly rebuilt to accommodate housing. Across the road, Charlton House at No. 571 was built in 1750, and the taller houses alongside some 20 years earlier.

A particularly significant landmark is the High Cross monument, an isolated memorial to one of Tottenham's ancient centres now surrounded by the one-way traffic system opposite Philip Lane. References to the High Cross date back to 1456, but its origins are obscure. It seems to have served as a waymark and a place where there was once a market, but its survival probably owes much to Dean Wood. Wood lived on the east side of the monument around 1580, when it was a column of wood supported by four spurs, with a square sheet of lead on top to throw off the water. Because it was decayed and rotten, it was taken down by Dean Wood

around 1600 and rebuilt as an octangular brick column, pointed at the top, with a weathercock. In 1809 it was given a stuccoed cladding.

In the east, the marshes have been saved from development, although there were many years of neglect and vandalism. During the 1960s they were used by the Council as a massive rubbish dump, and land was taken for a depot for the Victoria line and a major new road taking traffic from Tottenham Hale to Hertfordshire. The playground and sports grounds were lost and Tottenham's last farm, Asplins, was finally demolished in 1960.

The marshes were sold to the Lea Valley Park Authority in the 1960s, and although there was a difficult period when they were seen as a likely venue for a sports stadium, the area has weathered that stage and has since been restored and cared for. Bridges over the streams connect the different fields and a small wood shields the noise of the nearby road. Meadows, shrubs, trees and fields offer a natural environment for walkers and wildlife. At Stonebridge Lock a café, with canoe and bike hire, has become a centre for visitors, including the many travelling (or staying put) in their barges and houseboats. There are moments here when an older Tottenham can still be imagined.

152 *Greetings from Tottenham. A 1913 postcard showing the Wesleyan chapel, Bruce Castle, Prince of Wales Hospital and* Ferry Boat Inn.

BIBLIOGRAPHY

ABBREVIATIONS:
LBH   London Borough of Haringey
EH   Edmonton Hundred Historical Society
HHS   Hornsey Historical Society
TUDC   Tottenham Urban District Council
TBC   Tottenham Borough Council
TLM   Tottenham Libraries and Museums
LMAS   London and Middlesex Archaeological Society

GENERAL
Bedwell, William, *A Brief Description of the Towne of Tottenham High Cross in Middlesex* (1631, reprinted 1718)
Lord Coleraine, Henry, *The History of Tottenham*, H.G. Oldfield (1791)
Collicott, Sylvia L., *Connections: Haringey Local-National World Links*, Haringey Community Information
    Service (1986)
Fisk, Frederic, *A History of Tottenham* (1913)
Fisk, Frederic, *The History of the Ancient Parish of Tottenham*, 2nd series (1923)
Griffin, H.J., *Old Tottenham and Edmonton*, Crusha & Son Ltd (1926)
Murray, Ian, *Haringey Before Our Time*, HHS (1993)
Oldfield, H.G. and Dyson, R.R., *The History & Antiquities of Tottenham High Cross* (1790)
Oxford Dictionary of National Biography (on-line edition)
Pinching, Albert, *Wood Green Past*, Historical Publications (2000)
Pinching, Albert and Dell, David, *Haringey Hidden Streams Revealed*, HHS (2005)
Robinson, Wm, *The History & Antiquities of Tottenham*, 2nd edn (1840)
Roe, William James, *Ancient Tottenham* (1949)
Roe, William James, *Tottenham, Edmonton & Enfield Historical Notebook*, Percy Press (1952)
The Victoria History of the Counties of England, Volumes I & V (1976)

TOTTENHAM MANORIAL ROLLS
1318-77, translated by W. McB Marcham, TLM (1963)
1377-99, translated by R. Oram, TLM (1961)
1510-31, translated by W. McB Marcham, TLM (1960)
1531-46, translated by I.G. Murray, LBH Library, Museums & Arts Service (1975)
1547-58, translated by W. McB Marcham, TLM (1959)
1558-82, translated by W. McB Marcham, TLM (1963)

MEDIEVAL PERIOD
Avery, David, *Manorial Systems in the Edmonton Hundred in Late Medieval & Tudor Periods*, EH no.6 (1963)
Domesday Book (ed. John Morris, 1986)
Dorre, Stephen, *Domesday Book & and Origins of Edmonton Hundred*, EH no.48 (1986)
Moore, Margaret F., *The Lands of the Scottish Kings in England*, George Allen & Unwin Ltd (1915)
Moss, Douglas, 'The Economic Development of a Middlesex Village', *Agricultural History Review*, vol.28, part 2
    (1980)
Moss, Douglas and Murray, Ian, *15th Century Middlesex Terrier*, LMAS (1974)
Moss, Douglas and Murray, Ian, *Land & Labour in 14th Century Tottenham*, LMAS (1973)
Moss, Douglas and Murray, Ian, *Signs of Change in a Medieval Village Community*, LMAS (1976)

TUDOR/STUART PERIOD
Avery, D., *The Tudor Hundred of Edmonton: Evidence and Survivals*, EH, no.56 (1995)
Bolitho, J.R., *Tudor Tottenham*, EH, no.11 (1966)
Field Book of the 1619 Dorset Survey

EIGHTEENTH AND EARLY NINETEENTH CENTURY
Hoare, Eddie, *Eighteenth Century Tottenham*, EH, no.21 (1971)
Pollock, J., *Tottenham 1800-1850*, EH, no.29 (1974)
Richardson, S.I., *Edmonton Poor Law Union 1837-1854*, EH, no.12
Tottenham Vestry Minutes (1789)

NINETEENTH AND TWENTIETH CENTURIES
Barker, Kenneth, *How Rural Tottenham Disappeared* (2008)
Curtis, Peter, *In Times Past, Wood Green & Tottenham* (1991)
Harris, J.D., *Outrage: An Edwardian Tragedy* (2000)
Hawkes, H.G., *Tottenham Shops, A Personal Memory*, EH, no.46
Hill, Albert, *Seventy-two Years in Tottenham* (1899)
How Things Were: Growing Up in Tottenham 1890-1920, Tottenham History Workshop (1981)
Protz, Christine, *Tottenham, Haringey & Wood Green*, Sutton Publishing (1995)
Protz, Christine and Hedgecock, Deborah, *Tottenham & Wood Green Past & Present*, Sutton Publishing (2003)
The Story of the London Boroughs, Tottenham Past and Present, TUDC
The Urban Growth of Haringey, LBH Libraries, Museum & Art Service (1977)

EDUCATION
Coleraine Park Schools Log Books: 1881-1946
Robinson, Jean, *The History of Tottenham Grammar School*, EH (1979)
Willingly to School, LBH Catalogue (1970)

HISTORIC BUILDINGS AND HOUSING
Bruce Castle Museums & Park. Conservation Management Plan, Purcell Miller Triplan (2008)
Cherry, Bridget and Pevsner, Nikolaus, *The Buildings of England, London 4: North*, Penguin (2001)
Cooper, Nicholas, *Bruce Castle: A Historical Report*, LBH (2000)
The Englishman's Castle, LBH Catalogue (1974)
Hinshelwood, John, *Philanthropy & Speculation*, MA Thesis (2007)
History of Coombes Croft House, TUDC (1925)
Pegram, Jean, *From Manor House to Museum*, HHS
Saunders, Matthew, *Buildings of Tottenham*, EH (1976)

INDUSTRIAL AND COMMERCIAL
Burnby, J.G.L. and Robinson, A.E., *Now Turned into Fair Garden Plots*, EH (1983)
Lewis, Jim, *London's Lea Valley*, Phillimore (1999)

RELIGION AND CHARITIES
Collie, R., *The Quakers of Tottenham*, EH (1978)
Hawkes, H.G., *The Reynardsons & Their Almshouses*, EH (1980)

SPORT AND LEISURE
Brazier, Roy, *Tottenham Hotspur Football Club 1882-1952*, Tempus (2000)
Brazier, Roy, *Tottenham Hotspur Football Club since 1952*, Tempus (2003)
McAndrew, Marlene, *Lost Theatres of Haringey*, HHS (2007)
Time Off, LBH Catalogue (1972)
Whitehouse, Chris and Hazel, *Haringey Pubs*, Tempus (2004)

TRANSPORT
Burnby, J.G.L. and Parker, M., *Navigation of the River Lea, 1190-1780*, EH (1978)
Pam, D.O., *The Stamford Hill Green Lanes Turnpike Trust*, EH, part I (1963); part II (1965)
Transport through Time, LBH Exhibition Catalogue (1981)

WARTIME
Gough, T.W., *Wartime Letters from the Tottenham Home Front*, EH, no.54 (1994)
Hedgecock, Deborah and Waite, Robert, *Haringey at War*, Tempus (2004)

Index

Numbers in **bold** indicate illustrations.

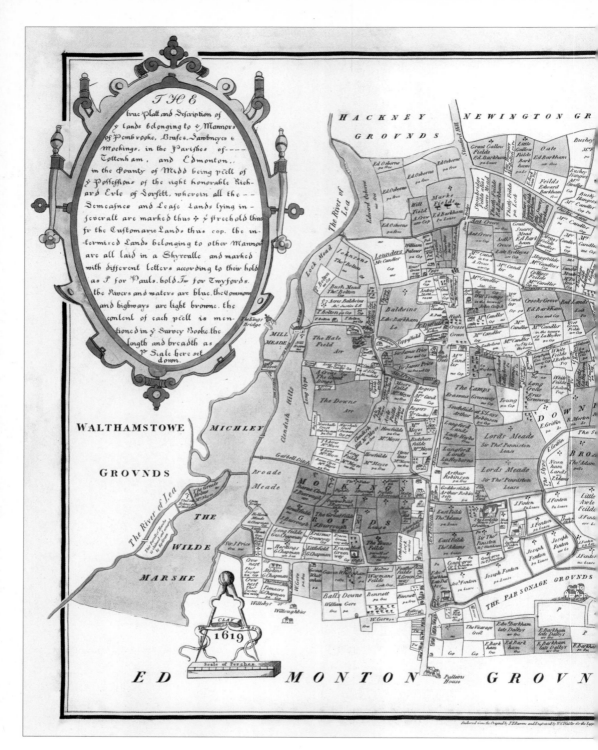